AmEuropa™

The Future of the West
and
The Next Superpower

A Short Introduction

Kent M. Chater

Author of
*AmEuropa: Love and Betrayal in the
Greatest Alliance of Nations*

Bloomington, IN      Milton Keynes, UK

authorHOUSE®

AuthorHouse™
1663 Liberty Drive, Suite 200
Bloomington, IN 47403
www.authorhouse.com
Phone: 1-800-839-8640

AuthorHouse™ UK Ltd.
500 Avebury Boulevard
Central Milton Keynes, MK9 2BE
www.authorhouse.co.uk
Phone: 08001974150

First published by AuthorHouse 3/19/2007

ISBN: 978-1-4343-0133-8 (sc)

Library of Congress Control Number: 2007901963

*Printed in the United States of America
Bloomington, Indiana*

This book is printed on acid-free paper.

AMEUROPA as well as the AmEuropean Flag

and Banner *are trademarks of Kent M. Chater. The
AmEuropean flag and banner were designed by
Kent M. Chater.*

Acknowledgments

I wish to express my gratitude and thanks to my mother Ella, Paula, and Sally for their support and proof-reading of the manuscript. I am also grateful to Paula for her cover design work. In addition, I would like to thank Rolf Hoppler for his support.

"Let us remember that our interest is in concord, not in conflict; and that our real eminence rests in the victories of peace, not those of war."

> **—William McKinley (1843-1901),**
> **the twenty-fifth U.S. President**
> **(1897-1901), assassinated**

"If we do not want to die together in war, we must learn to live together in peace."

> **—Harry Truman (1884-1972),**
> **the thirty-third U.S. President**
> **(1945–1953)**

« Nous ne coalisons pas des Etats, nous unissons des hommes. » (We do not form coalitions of States; we unite people.)[1]

> **—Jean Monnet (1888–1979),**
> **architect of the European Union**

CONTENTS

Introduction

Americans and Canadians, imagine yourselves living in exciting London, Paris, or Berlin with an exquisite view of the London Bridge, Eiffel Tower, or Brandenburg Gate from your charming home or office. Europeans and Canadians, imagine yourselves working in electrifying New York, San Francisco, or Seattle with a magnificent view of the Statue of Liberty, the Golden Gate Bridge, or the Space Needle from your cozy home or office. And if you prefer the beach to the city, imagine yourselves lying in the warm sun along the picturesque coast of one of the Canary Islands or the Costa de Sol in Spain or along the scenic coast of Miami Beach or Southern California in America. This is the kind of life, the kind of freedom that AmEuropa shall create for you.

This AmEuropean manifesto is a non-fictional explanation of my concept and vision of AmEuropa, which I first introduced to the world in my novel *AmEuropa: Love and Betrayal in the Greatest Alliance of Nations.*[2] The word "AmEuropa" is a contraction of the continents of North America and Europe.

In this short introduction to AmEuropa, I shall put forth a vision of the future, a blueprint for a better world, a world of greater peace with increased individual liberty and personal freedom. I do so in the name of liberty and freedom and for peace and the survival of civilizations. It is today that we create tomorrow; hence, I call for AmEuropean unity today so that it may become a reality tomorrow.

I shall provide the reader with a political overview of the Alliance of AmEuropa, the future of the West, and the next superpower. I shall introduce the reader to the principles of AmEuropean unity, the AmEuropean Greater Common Market, the AmEuropean Area of Freedom, the AmEuropean Movement, AmEuropeanism, AmEuropean cosmopolitanism, and AmEuropean integration, all of which support and promote the concept of AmEuropa as well as peace, liberty, and freedom. In addition, I shall provide the reader with answers to the following questions: What is AmEuropa? What is the purpose of AmEuropa? How does AmEuropa benefit corporations, small businesses, and the common citizen? Why does AmEuropa benefit the West and the world? How is AmEuropa a superpower? And why is AmEuropa necessary?

« Un jour viendra où la guerre vous paraîtra aussi absurde et aussi impossible entre Paris et Londres, entre Pétersbourg et Berlin [qu']entre Rouen et Amiens, entre Boston et Philadelphie. Un jour viendra où vous, France, vous Russie, vous Italie, vous Angleterre, vous Allemagne […] vous vous fondrez étroitement dans une unité supérieure, et vous constituerez la fraternité européenne. »	A day will come when war seems as absurd and as impossible between Paris and London, between Saint Petersburg and Berlin as between Rouen and Amiens, between Boston and Philadelphia. A day will come when you, France, you Russia, you England, you Germany… shall melt narrowly into one superior unity and constitute European fraternity.
—Victor Hugo, Discours inaugural du congrès de la Paix, 21 août 1849[3]	—Victor Hugo, Inaugural Discourse of the Peace Congress, 21 August 1849 (translated by Kent M. Chater)

Just as Victor Hugo's vision of a united Europe has become a reality, a united AmEuropa, shall too one day become a reality. Already in 1849, Victor Hugo believed in the future friendship and unity of the United States of America and the United States of Europe, as he wrote:

« Un jour viendra où l'on verra ces deux groupes immenses, les Etats-Unis d'Amérique, les Etats-Unis d'Europe, placés en face l'un de l'autre, se tendant la main par-dessus les mers! »
—Victor Hugo, Discours inaugural du congrès de la Paix, 1849[4]

A day will come when we shall see these two immense groups, the United States of America, the United States of Europe, situated across from one another, shaking hands above the seas.
—Victor Hugo, Inaugural Discourse of the Congress of Peace, 1849

(translation by Kent M. Chater)

In AmEuropa, Americans and Canadians shall be permitted to live and work amid the marvels of old-world Europe. Their businesses, big or small, shall be allowed to freely open affiliate offices in Europe without any foreign restrictions. Likewise, Britons and Europeans shall be permitted to live and work amongst the beauty of new-world America and Canada. Their businesses, big or small, shall be allowed to freely open affiliate offices in America and Canada without any foreign restrictions. As a Berliner can now live and work in Madrid, a Londoner in Paris, and a Roman in Dublin, so too shall an American be allowed to work in Vancouver and Paris and a Canadian and European in New York and San Francisco.

The Europeans and the peoples of the Caribbean have built their own single and common markets. Moreover, the Africans, the Asians, and six of the Persian Gulf countries have begun work on building their own free trade zones and common markets. Now it is time for the Atlantic alliance—that is the North Atlantic Treaty Organization (NATO)—to build a common market. AmEuropa is the rational middle road between two extremes: those wishing to have open borders and those wishing to have closed borders. If Turkey with ninety-five percent of its landmass outside of Europe can be considered for entry into the European Union (a union of European states), then there is no logical reason to prevent the United States of America, Canada, and the European Union from building the Alliance of AmEuropa in which the free movement of goods, services, capital, and citizens is permitted and encouraged while retaining border controls wherever desired. "There is no reason," wrote U.S. Ambassador Schnabel to the EU, "why Europeans and Americans cannot debate and disagree, as different political constituencies do in the U.S., while recognizing and reaffirming the overarching framework of Western civilization that contains us all."[5]

Samuel Huntington, the chairman of the Harvard Academy for International and Area Studies, defines the West and Western civilization as being "...Europe, North America, plus other European settler countries such as Australia and New Zealand.... In the modern era, Western civilization is Euroamerican or North Atlantic civilization.... European-American civilization is, however, universally referred to as Western civilization."[6] AmEuropa incorporates that which Huntington calls "Euroamerican," "North Atlantic," or "European-American civilization." This Euroamerican, North Atlantic, or European-American civilization I call AmEuropean civilization. The term "the West" more or less refers to Western civilization and its free democracies.

In a new "global village" in which economic markets are tied and civilizations have clashed, European problems are North American problems and North American problems are European problems. With the many forces of hate presently exercising their will against the West, it is urgent that the nations of the West strengthen their solidarity; for divided, the West cannot stand!

Instead of deepening its counterweight against the United States (U.S.), the European Union (EU) should work on improving its relations with the U.S. by freely accepting Americans and Canadians to live and work in Europe. The EU only needs a new mission—go west! "Go west!" rather than east can once again become a motto. Similarly, instead of acting unilaterally, thereby alienating itself, the U.S. could improve its relations with the EU by freely accepting EU citizens to live and work in the US.

The date of the founding of the Alliance of AmEuropa, also referred to as simply "AmEuropa" or "the Alliance," shall depend upon whether people's actions are led predominantly by emotion or by reason. If people's actions are led predominantly by emotion, then the Alliance of AmEuropa may not become a reality until after a dreadful adversity or horrifying disaster unites the people of the West. If, however, people prove to be led predominantly by reason then the Alliance of AmEuropa will exist prior to a devastating blow to the West. To achieve peace, it is wiser to prevent acts of violence than to retaliate with acts of violence in the name of "justice" or "preventive war." "Preventive war," Chomsky writes, "falls within the category of war crimes."[7] For this reason, AmEuropa is to be built in peace, through peace, and for peace, as

AmEuropa procures peace through the strength and strength through unity.

The West has two options—unity or downfall, unity in AmEuropa or downfall in the status quo. Only through AmEuropa can the West remain a world leader and stay head of China or at least keep parity with it. In finally recognizing this truth, the West shall unite in AmEuropa. The widening gap between America and Europe since the fall of the Soviet Union, endangering the West and the world shall be nipped in the bud before it is too late.

This widening gap is detrimental to the survival of Western civilization. The wider the gap, the weaker the West and the greater the instability: division is weakness and unity is strength. Division renders the West less secure and the world more dangerous. Unity renders the West more secure and the world safer. Hence, we have good reason to ensure the unity of AmEuropeans. Furthermore, the integration of peoples not only ensures the cooperation of their governments but also extends the liberties and freedoms of their peoples.

With the fall of the Soviet Union, the common threat of the West disappeared but only to be replaced by new enemies of the West. The emergence of these new enemies must unite the West, not divide the West. "One clear result of the unification of Europe is that the gap between the two sides of the Atlantic Ocean is growing wider every day."[8] As the U.S. has used military force unilaterally without U.N. approval and EU endorsement, some EU politicians wish to make a superpower out of the EU in order to be a "counterweight" to American power and supremacy. Kagan, the senior associate at the Carnegie Endowment for International Peace and director of the U.S. Leadership Project, points out, "It is true that the Bush administration came into office with something of a chip on its shoulder. The realist-nationalist impulses it inherited from the Republican Congress of the 1990s made it appear almost eager to scorn the opinions of much of the rest of the world. The picture it painted in its early months was of a behemoth thrashing about against constraints that only it could see."[9] Similarly, Francis Fukuyama, director of the International Development Program at the School of Advanced International Studies at John Hopkins University, writes, "The United States... has provoked a great deal on unity among normally fractious Europeans around the view that the irresponsible exercise of American power is one of the chief problems in contemporary politics."[10]

The "counterweight thesis," that a united Europe should become a superpower to match the United States, is not only counterproductive but also detrimental not only for the survival of the West but also for the survival of civilizations and the world. In the same way, the United States acting alone, unilaterally without the endorsement of the United Nations and without the support of the EU, alienates America and threatens world peace and the existence of the West. Divisive-mindedness and peer competition can lead to alienation and discord, which in turn can lead to trade wars, division, dissension, and conflict, first economically, then politically, and then militarily. The unity of the West is life-oriented; the division of the West into two camps—European and American—is death-oriented. The integration of AmEuropean citizens and AmEuropean economies prevents alienation, discord, division, dissension, and conflict among AmEuropean member countries and brings about their cooperation and partnership. Survival of the West depends not upon creating two superpowers but upon deepening the Atlantic alliance. The survival of the West depends not upon competition but upon cooperation, not upon dissension but friendship, not upon division but partnership, and not upon alienation but integration. In the end, the survival of the West shall depend upon its solidarity and skill to unite in the Alliance of AmEuropa.

Switzerland is an outstanding example of a nation with many cultures and official languages living and working together in unity and harmony. The minor cultural and governmental differences between Western countries do not merit disunity and should not arouse discord. Having studied at the University of Fribourg, an officially bilingual French and German university in Fribourg, Switzerland, an officially bilingual French and German city, in an officially multilingual country (German, French, Italian, and Rhaeto-Romanic) for almost seven years, I have experienced many cultures with different spoken and written official languages living and working harmoniously together for the common good of the whole.

There is no need to be scared of people from other cultures who speak a different language. You would be surprised to find out how much you really have in common. "As Western countries," writes Samuel Huntington, "increasingly interact with increasingly powerful non-Western societies, they become more and more aware of their common Western cultural core that binds them together. Leaders from both sides of the Atlantic have emphasized the need to rejuvenate the Atlantic community."[11]

Rockwell A. Schnabel, former U.S. Ambassador to the European Union, warns us against the weakening of the Atlantic alliance:

"Not only Europe and America stand to lose from a weakening of the Atlantic alliance; so does the rest of world. The U.S. and the EU working together are a tremendous force for good: alleviating poverty, hunger, and disease; defending human rights; and increasing the possibilities for wealth creation through economic freedom. But if our cooperation breaks down, the losses will be incalculable, especially since these opportunities may not be ours for long....

As Lord Patten put it ... the U.S. and the EU have two decades left to 'shape the world' in the ways we deem best. After that, in his estimation, economic and demographic trends will force us to share that power with the two emerging Asian giants.... Meaning that now is the Atlantic moment, the moment of America and Europe. Will we seize it?"[12]

The Alliance of AmEuropa is the answer to "Will we seize it?" as well as to "How will we seize it?"

In the twenty-first century, AmEuropa shall usher in, what I have called in my novel *AmEuropa: Love and Betrayal in the Greatest Alliance of Nations,* the "Age of Amity": the age of friendship among Western nations in which partnership and integration reign over divisive-mindedness and alienation.[13] With AmEuropa, the age of separation shall be over and the Age of Amity shall have begun. AmEuropa, as a contraction of North America and Europe, stands for inclusiveness, solidarity, and unity.

Since the tragedy of September 11, the civil liberties of North Americans and Europeans have been eroding, pleasing no one but the enemies of liberty, freedom, and the West. It is now time for the West to take two steps forward. It is time to defy the enemies of the West by advancing our liberties and freedoms, as our forefathers in both North America and Europe had done for us. Now is the time to build the AmEuropean Greater Common Market and the AmEuropean Area of Freedom.[14] Now is the time for AmEuropean unity. Now is the time for AmEuropa!

Chapter 1
What is AmEuropa?

AmEuropa, short for the Alliance of AmEuropa, shall be an alliance supporting the solidarity of the nations of the Atlantic alliance (NATO) as well as the nations of North America and Europe. AmEuropa shall be a deeper forging of the Atlantic alliance not only to give it a renewed sense of purpose but also to give its citizens something that would benefit them directly through the establishment of the AmEuropean Greater Common Market and the AmEuropean Area of Freedom.

AmEuropa shall be a transatlantic alliance. As such, its government shall be supranational and multinational; its people, multinational and multiracial; its cultural and technological tradition, Western; and its citizenship, AmEuropean. AmEuropean citizenship shall not replace but complement an individual's national citizenship.

AmEuropa shall allow the free movement of goods, capital, services, and citizens (those holding citizenship of an Alliance member country regardless of race, creed, color, sexual orientation, or class) among member countries between North America and Europe. Hence, AmEuropa shall be an alliance with a greater common market and an area of freedom.

When referring to countries within the European Union, I use the customary EU-term "member states"; and when referring to countries within AmEuropa, I use the term "member countries." For the free movement of goods, services, capital, and citizens, I use the term "citizens" and not "persons" or "people," for only citizens (those holding citizenship of an Alliance member country) would be afforded the right to live and work in any member country. Furthermore, the term "accession" means "the process of joining the European Union."[15] Hence, with reference to AmEuropa, I shall use the term "accession" to signify the process of joining the Alliance of AmEuropa.

Specifically, AmEuropa shall be an alliance of the United States of America, Canada, and the European Union. Hence, AmEuropa would consist of the United States of America, Canada, plus twenty-five of the twenty-seven member states of the EU, equaling twenty-seven member countries. Although Bulgaria and Romania joined the EU on January 1, 2007, not all EU member states will grant Bulgarians and Romanians the right to live and work in their states for some time to come. Not until Bulgarians and Romanians are granted the right to live and work in all EU member states would Bulgaria and Romania meet the preliminary requirements for accession into the Alliance of AmEuropa.

Each member country of AmEuropa shall be free to retain border controls wherever desired. The Alliance of AmEuropa, bearing the classification of an "alliance" and not a "union," shall permit the continuance of border controls between member countries desiring such, in particular between Canada and the United States and between North America and Europe as an important deterrent and hindrance to terrorism.

Politically, AmEuropa, as a transatlantic alliance, shall be the middle road between a world divided into separate governing nations and a world united under one supreme government. Each member nation shall be free to develop its own concept of state and government. Economically, AmEuropa with its Greater Common Market and Area of Freedom shall offer AmEuropeans a freedom of choice: the freedom to choose between the American, Canadian or European way of life in any member country that best embodies the individual's desired concept of state and government. AmEuropeans shall be free to choose the AmEuropean social, state and governmental system as well as the national and regional culture that best fit their character and lifestyle.

"...The institution of war must be abolished, and this involves also abolishing the institution of local sovereignty, since wars are waged by local sovereign states, and local states are likely to continue to go to war with each other so long as they retain the sovereign right to do so," wrote renowned English historian Arnold J. Toynbee.[16] "The old realist model," writes Fukuyama, "of international relations that sees the world exclusively organized around sovereign nation-states simply does not correspond to the world that is emerging, and it will not be sufficient to meet the needs of legitimacy and effectiveness in international action in the future.... Many Europeans ... distrust sovereignty per se because they believe it is a source of conflict and war, based on their experiences during two world wars...."[17] The integration of AmEuropean peoples and economies shall compel

AmEuropean governments to cooperate in partnership, thereby reducing the possibility of conflict and war.

The creation of AmEuropa, unifying Americans, Canadians, Britons, and Europeans—collectively called "AmEuropeans"—in a nonfederal, non-centralized alliance, is to be achieved peacefully, thus demonstrating to the world the West's commitment to democracy, equality, individual liberty, personal freedom, and world peace.

Any cultural, political or economic differences that arise between the governments of the U.S., Canada, and the member states of the EU do not merit denying their citizens the right to live and work in each other's countries in the twenty first century, the Age of Amity. The sharing of ideas and lifestyles among these member nations would not cause a cultural clash, as these countries are part of Western civilization. Sharing would bring forth an enriching experience and speed up progress in the West. America, Canada, and Europe need each other to ensure not only the survival of their nations and cultures but also to ensure the survival of the West and the world.

The Swiss Confederation, that is Switzerland; the Commonwealth of Nations, formerly called the British Commonwealth, including bilingual Canada; the United States of America; the Atlantic Charter signed by Roosevelt and Churchill; the North Atlantic Treaty Organization (NATO); the Franco-German Cooperation; the North American Free Trade Area (NAFTA); the European Union (EU); and the Transatlantic Economic Partnership (TEP) are precursors of AmEuropa. In addition, the goal of the TransAtlantic Business Dialogue (TABD) "is to help establish a Barrier-Free Transatlantic Market ... which will stimulate innovation and economic growth, more investment and create new jobs."[18] Nevertheless, as

NATO, also called the Atlantic alliance, is the bulwark of the West, it is out of this alliance that AmEuropa shall be born. NATO unites countries; AmEuropa unites people.[19]

For the general public, terms such as TEP and NATO sound like business organizations, whereas AmEuropa sounds like a nation or superpower, uniting not only businesses and countries but also and more importantly people. It is to be remembered that people are more important than material things. The love for people should be at the forefront of politics and not only commerce, wealth, and power.

AmEuropa cannot be viewed as an extension of the European Union, for that would suggest that the Alliance member countries be under the jurisdiction of Brussels, the capital of the European Union; that is not the aim. Hence, AmEuropa is to be an alliance, not a union, confederacy, or federation. There shall be no central, federal government. Member countries and the EU shall be free to preserve their sovereignty and autonomy. Each nation-state shall be free to accept the terms it desires and opt out of those it does not with the exception of the four freedoms. The AmEuropean four freedoms are the free movement of goods, services, capital, and citizens among member countries of AmEuropa while retaining border controls wherever desired.[20] All member countries must accept the four freedoms, as they form the basis and spirit of unity, unifying the nations of AmEuropa. AmEuropean integration, which includes the four freedoms, is a core principle of the Alliance of AmEuropa.

The Alliance of AmEuropa shall be primarily economic, partially political, and not militaristic. AmEuropa with a population of approximately 818 million people

(EU 487 million, U.S. 298 million, and Canada 33 million) shall stretch across twenty-seven countries on two continents.[21] Moreover, with a 2006 purchasing power parity Gross Domestic Product of $26.97 trillion (U.S. $12.98 trillion, EU $12.82 trillion, and Canada $1.17 trillion) out of a Gross World Product of $65 trillion AmEuropa shall account for approximately forty percent of the world's income, making it the world's most powerful economy and richest common market with the world's two largest exporters: Germany ($1.133 trillion) and America ($974 billion).[22]

Nearly all of the planned founding member countries of the Alliance of AmEuropa are presently members of the North Atlantic Treaty Organization (NATO). It is NATO, however, and not the Alliance that shall be responsible for the defense of AmEuropa, for the purpose of AmEuropa is peace and the extension of individual liberty and personal freedom. The Alliance of AmEuropa—exemplifying partnership, cooperation, and integration—shall be a world unifier, a nucleus for world peace.

As admission to the Alliance shall be voluntary and democratic, all nation-states must wish to join the Alliance, and they must be accepted by all other nation-states in the Alliance. Alliance membership shall never to be forced upon any nation; AmEuropa is to be constructed through democratic means.

The founding members of the Alliance of AmEuropa shall be the United States of America, Canada, and the European Union, including twenty-five of its twenty-seven member states. The EU member states to be simultaneously Alliance member countries are Austria, Belgium, Cyprus, Czech Republic, Denmark, Estonia,

Finland, France, Germany, Greece, Hungary, Ireland, Italy, Latvia, Lithuania, Luxembourg, Malta, Poland, Portugal, the Netherlands, Slovakia, Slovenia, Spain, Sweden, and the United Kingdom.

AmEuropa is the core of the West and together with NATO its bulwark. AmEuropa and NATO, together, are the protectors of Western values, mores, and virtues, including democracy, equality, freedom, liberty, peace, security, and the rule of law.[23]

The most important step to AmEuropean unity is the creation of the Alliance of AmEuropa with its AmEuropean Greater Common Market (a great single domestic free-trade market in which internal trade quotas and tariffs are abolished) and its AmEuropean Area of Freedom (the area in which the free movement of goods, services, capital and citizens—collectively known as the "four freedoms"—is permitted and encouraged among the twenty-seven member countries of the Alliance).

Technically, the Alliance of AmEuropa may be regarded as having a common market as opposed to a single market, for to some a single market implies a deepening toward federalism and the removal of border controls, which is not the case in AmEuropa. AmEuropa is not federalist in nature: that is to say, AmEuropa shall not have a central, federal government.

The Alliance of AmEuropa shall enhance individual liberty and personal freedom by according AmEuropeans a larger geopolitical realm in which to fulfill their desires. This larger geopolitical realm provides AmEuropeans with more opportunities to fulfill their desires for recognition, happiness, and success in whatever their undertakings; to satisfy their cultural, material, and spiritual needs; and to develop their creative self-expression. In sum, AmEuropa empowers the individual's pursuit of happiness.

There shall be no supranational currency union as in the EU. Nation-states in the Alliance and the EU shall retain the right to determine their own currency and remain free to adjust their own exchange and interest rates. Each nation-state shall also retain the right to establish and develop its own form of state and government as long as it respects human rights, equality, and is "founded on the principles of democracy, individual liberty and the rule of law."[24] This right also includes the right for any nation-state to retain border controls.

The supranational governmental agencies and bureaus of AmEuropa shall be dispersed among its member countries, thereby affording all member countries the opportunity to benefit from the increased employment benefits of the Alliance. Alliance agencies and bureaus shall be dispersed among member countries, equally between North America and Europe. By dispersing the AmEuropean agencies and bureaus throughout AmEuropa, a blow to any one AmEuropean city through either a natural disaster or a terrorist attack could not destroy the organization and administration of the entire Alliance. In other words, AmEuropa shall not have all its eggs in one basket.

AmEuropa, as an alliance of nations, shall facilitate and foster intergovernmental cooperation, peace, and stability as a collective whole and empower its individual nation-states by affording each nation the right to veto, thereby giving each nation-state a say as to the development of not only its own nation-state but also the Alliance of AmEuropa and the world.

The West is to lead by example. By creating the Alliance of AmEuropa, the West shall exemplify cooperation, partnership, solidarity, and teamwork, all of which are essential for world peace.

As strength is afforded by unity and unity is accorded by alliance, this great alliance with its vast common market shall increase strength, galvanize cooperative and peaceful relations among member nations, spur economic growth, and extend the freedom of movement of all its citizens. The AmEuropean Greater Common Market shall spur economic growth by stimulating free trade between two commensurate and economically balanced continents and by lowering consumer prices through greater competition. Furthermore, the vast common market shall increase business opportunities not only for corporations but also for hitherto disadvantaged small businesses, the self-employed, and the individual. Small businesses shall be able to expand more easily into new markets and open up affiliate offices in any Alliance member country. Corporations and small businesses alike shall be able to hire employees from any member country of the Alliance. In addition, the common citizen of an Alliance member country shall be able to apply for a job in any member country and be hired without all the bureaucratic red tape that is presently required, which prevents the common citizen from working legally in a foreign country. AmEuropa shall remove the bureaucratic red tape for corporations, small businesses, and citizens alike. That is democratic equality on a grand scale. The AmEuropean Area of Freedom shall extend the freedom of movement of AmEuropeans by affording them the right to live and to work anywhere within the borders of any of its twenty-seven member countries.

The purpose of AmEuropa shall be to advance peace, create unity, increase prosperity, security, and stability as well as to extend individual liberty and personal freedom. Thus, the greatness of AmEuropa shall lie in the spirit of its people, a spirit of goodness, love, and solidarity that unites people for greater liberty, freedom, equality, and peace. In many ways, AmEuropa is the long awaited fruition of the rational, cosmopolitan and unifying ideals sowed by the philosophers, dramatists, poets, thinkers, and writers of the Enlightenment period of the seventeenth and eighteenth centuries. In AmEuropean politics, the light of enlightenment and reason shall reign supreme over the darkness of ignorance and fanaticism.

"Overall the growing economic strength of the Asian countries renders them increasingly immune to Western pressure concerning human rights and democracy," writes Samuel Huntington.[25] Unity is strength! Hence, only through AmEuropean unity can the West effectively champion human rights as well as prevent China—one of the world's most repressive societies[26]—and its authoritarian communistic government from becoming the next superpower and world leader. The strength afforded by AmEuropean unity shall keep the West a step ahead of China. Moreover, AmEuropean unity shall prevent the fall of the West for at least a half millennium by revitalizing its creativity, culture, and strength.

Americans and Europeans working together can more effectively help not only themselves but also the world. Hence, the purpose of AmEuropa is to improve relations between North America and Europe, thereby reversing the trend of a widening gap between America and Europe that has been occurring since the fall of the Soviet Union. AmEuropa shall revitalize NATO (the

Atlantic alliance), improve relations among the nations of the Atlantic alliance, and increase the individual liberty, personal freedom, prosperity, and security of the nations of the Atlantic alliance, especially those nations contributing to the defense of the West and the free world.

For the aforementioned goals to come to pass, a closer alliance, bringing the peoples of North America and Europe together, is required. Furthermore, the purpose of AmEuropa is to create a nucleus for world peace and to set an example of cooperation and partnership among nations on a global scale.

Europeans and Americans have been working together in NATO for almost 60 years; hence, it is time to let the citizens who have been paying for NATO benefit in visible and tangible terms of increased trade and greater mobility, thereby increasing their prosperity, personal freedom, and employment opportunities. Reintegrating the peoples of North America and Europe and their economies would ensure the cooperation of peoples, businesses, and their governments, thereby reversing the trend of a "widening gap" and alleviating trade wars—blunders that if left unchecked could ignite into more perilous conflicts, cold or hot.

Without AmEuropean unity and AmEuropean integration, the European Union benefits Europe in some ways to the detriment of America, making the EU and the euro counterweights to both American supremacy and the American dollar. It would be a considerable blow to the U.S. dollar and the U.S. economy if the euro were to replace the U.S. dollar as the world reserve currency

In AmEuropa, AmEuropeans shall see gains in individual liberty, personal freedom, economic growth, and employment opportunities. The free movement of goods, capital, services, and citizens among twenty-seven or more AmEuropean countries shall lower prices and increase product variety for consumers by increasing competition. Furthermore, the free movement of citizens shall be a tremendous boost for the service and transportation industries as well as for smaller businesses and the individual. North American and European companies and individuals shall have access to the two vast markets of the two largest economies in the world, thereby increasing commerce between North America and Europe.

With the recent cuts in Employee benefits and salaries (at the airlines for example as a result of September 11), coupled with inflation and the loss of civil liberties due to acts of terrorism, the common citizen in North America and Europe is long overdue for a gain in individual liberty and personal freedom. A gain in liberty and freedom would show the enemies of the West that their threats and acts of destruction have failed and that the West is in essence winning the war against terrorism.

What is the gain in liberty and freedom that would benefit the common citizen that shows terrorists that the West cannot be threatened into giving up its civil liberties and that it is actually winning the war against terrorism? This personal gain benefiting the common citizen would be the granting of four freedoms: the free movement of goods, services, capital, and, most importantly, citizens between North America and Europe. The psychology is such: the more the terrorists hate liberty and freedom and try to take them away, the more we create liberty and freedom. The more they try to divide Europe from America, the more we unite Europe and America. To win the war against terrorism we must forge solidarity and create freedom, that is to say new freedoms that benefit the economy, business, and the individual alike. Since the second Iraq war, the gap between Europe and America has widened faster and greater then ever only to benefit the enemies of the West. The enemies of the West have apparently learned more from Napoleon's famous battle plan "Divide and conquer!" than the West. "Divide and conquer" was his renowned battle plan, which never failed him until the allied powers had become smart enough not to let themselves be divided both strategically and tactically. To conquer the enemy you have to divide them first, so how can the West commit such a blunder as to let itself be divided. If the enemies of the West learn that they can play America and Europe against each other, then neither will remain a superpower for long. World peace is only obtainable if North America and Europe show themselves united to the rest of the world and especially in the face of their enemies—the enemies of the West. When two argue the third laughs: when America and Europe argue, the enemies of the West laugh. Solidarity of the West is AmEuropa; strength through AmEuropean unity is the Alliance. A widening gap between North America and Europe is exactly what the enemies of the West desire. They want to see the West divided, for to defeat the West, you have to divide it first. Hence, AmEuropa was conceived to reverse the widening gap between Europe and America as well as to extend the freedoms of Alliance member nations.

Stringent U.S. immigration laws since 1995, restricting legal immigration into the U. S. to 675,000 persons per year, prevent most citizens of the Atlantic alliance from moving to the United States. The requirements to be one of these 675,000 persons per year are difficult to fulfill.[27] In short, an applicant wishing to immigrate legally to America must fulfill one of the following requirements:

1. An applicant must be married to an American citizen, thereby putting same-sex couples at a grave disadvantage.
2. Or an applicant must have an American citizen in the immediate family who has earned over $24,000 dollars a year for at least three years and is willing to sponsor the applicant.
3. Or an applicant must invest between $500,000 and $1,000,000 U.S. dollars, depending on the location, and employ at least ten unrelated people.
4. Or an applicant must be offered employment in the U.S. but then "must obtain certification from the Department of Labor that there are no qualified workers available for the proposed employment in the U.S."[28]
5. Or an applicant must win the Diversity Immigrant Visa Lottery. Good luck!

Immigration the other way from America to Canada or from America to Europe is not much easier.

The nations of the West profess to be nations of liberty and freedom; yet the common citizen of North America lives confined within the frontiers of his or her nation-state, and the common citizen of Europe lives either confined within his or her nation-state or within the frontiers of the EU or Schengen signatory states. Furthermore, people of the same sex have been denied the right to marry in most Western countries except in Belgium, Canada, Spain, and the Netherlands. Same-sex couples of different nationalities are forced to live separated in their respective nation-states or in the EU for some Europeans. This is not democratic, as it does not equate to the free and egalitarian principles that we, in democratic nations of the West, profess. AmEuropean freedom of movement helps to keep couples and loved ones, whether straight or gay; entire families, not only immediate family members; and friends together, for all AmEuropeans shall have the right to live and work in any member country of AmEuropa.

With AmEuropa, the U.S. and EU can remain superpowers while furthering world peace. "Peace is an unmistakable equilibrium, which can be preserved only by acknowledged supremacy or equal power," explained renowned American historians Will and Ariel Durant.[29] The Alliance of AmEuropa is both: equal power among member nations of the Alliance and, due to its sheer size and strength, acknowledged supremacy by nonmember nations. Peace can be achieved through the strength of unity without actually having to use it. AmEuropa procures peace through strength and strength through unity. "Speak softly and carry a big stick," says the African proverb, borrowed by Theodore Roosevelt in 1901. The Alliance of AmEuropa is a prerequisite for world peace. The strength of unity achieved by the countries of the West in NATO during the Cold War was a strong enough deterrent to halt one of the greatest powers in history, the Soviet Union and the Warsaw Pact countries.

AmEuropa shall benefit the people and businesses of NATO countries, as they receive something back for the enormous outpouring of tax monies to build the massive armies and expensive weaponry for NATO. The people and businesses did gain in that the Cold War never did turn hot, but for the average citizen that is an elusive, intangible gain. With AmEuropa, people shall be able to see and experience something tangible for their money.

Since September 11, the citizens of North America and Europe have been loosing their civil liberties and have been traveling less causing airlines to declare bankruptcy. In addition, Western governments have been imposing ever increasingly stringent immigration policies that adversely affect the citizens of NATO member countries. The West has taken one step backward; now it is time to take two steps forward toward progress, peace, and greater liberty and freedom.

If AmEuropeans continue not only to travel less but also to immigrate less both ways across the Atlantic, then the cultural, economic, and intellectual circulatory system of Western civilization and the Atlantic alliance will become restricted and partially blocked. Like the human body, no part or nation-state of the West can survive for long if isolated from the rest. As separated entities, the West not only becomes decisively weakened politically, economically, and culturally but also less secure; consequently, the world becomes more dangerous.

To be healthy and flourish, the circulatory system of the West needs to be improved; this includes facilitating access to each other's markets in the West not only for commerce but also for citizens. In the end, it is life that counts, not things—the advancement of life in civilization, not the withdrawal of life from civilization. If the member countries of the West isolate themselves and their citizens due to the fear of terrorism or any other reason, the enemies of the West will believe that they are defeating the West and hastening its fall. AmEuropa provides the West with a goal and a path to follow out of its state of fear, frustration, and loss of direction.

In an essay entitled *Europe and NATO: Saving the Alliance,* Jeffrey Gedmin, the executive director of the New Atlantic initiative and a resident scholar at the American Enterprise Institute, calls for strong and common institutions if the Atlantic community is to have a future.

"When NATO was created half a century ago, British foreign secretary Ernest Bevin understood that it was more than a military alliance. He suggested that a successful alliance would also organize, mobilize, and encapsulate 'the ethical and spiritual forces of Western civilization.' Czech President Vaclav Havel has tried to make the same point today, arguing that the alliance should be seen as 'a guarantor of Euro-American civilization and thus as a pillar of global security.' If the Atlantic community is to have a future, then NATO and the Atlantic idea must be given new momentum. Americans and Europeans must reach an agreement that something called the West still exists, that it needs strong and common institutions, and that it is worthy of a serious and vigorous defense. This will require, above all, new leadership from Washington that is even-handed and is exercised in the service of shared transatlantic principles. Only this course will succeed in dampening European calls for 'emancipation' from the U.S. and in countering America's isolationist impulses."[30]

AmEuropa, as a deepening of NATO, shall be the "guarantor" of the West and "pillar of global security." It shall give the "Atlantic idea new momentum" and create "strong and common institutions," thereby strengthening the Atlantic community and thus "global security."

In AmEuropa, the EU does not compete against the U.S., and the U.S. does not compete against the EU. Both the U.S. and the EU, as pillars of AmEuropa, work together in each other's interest. In AmEuropa, the U.S. remains a superpower, and the EU attains its sought after status of superpower: two superpowers, one alliance.

History has taught us that the peaceful integration of national economies into a greater single internal domestic common market spurs economic growth and increases security, stability, and prosperity. The free movement of people, goods, services, and capital has proven to be effective. Hence, more and more countries are moving toward free-trade markets, common markets, and single markets. The following are examples of such markets:

1. The European Union (EU) consists of twenty-seven member states.
2. The European Economic Area (EEA) embraces twenty-five of the twenty-seven member states of the EU as well as Norway, Iceland, and Liechtenstein.
3. The European Free Trade Association (EFTA) is comprised of Norway, Iceland, Lichtenstein, and Switzerland.
4. The Schengen Agreement grants the free movement of persons without border controls among implementing signatory countries. Currently, out of thirty European signatory countries, fifteen

have already implemented the agreement by abolishing border controls between Schengen countries. The current agreement implementing countries are Belgium (1995), France (1995), Germany (1995), Luxembourg (1995), the Netherlands (1995), Portugal (1995), Spain (1995), Italy (1997), Austria (1997), Greece (2000), Denmark (2001), Finland (2001), Iceland (2001), Norway, (2001), Sweden (2001). All these countries except Norway and Iceland are EU members.

5. The North American Free Trade Area (NAFTA) is comprised of the United States of America, Canada, and Mexico.

6. The Caribbean Community and Common Market (CARICOM) consists of fifteen full members and five associate members.

7. The Caricom Single Market and Economy (CSME) includes thirteen countries.

8. The proposed "ASEAN [Association of Southeast Asian Nations] Free Trade Area" (AFTA) is to consist of the ASEAN-6: Brunei Darussalam, Indonesia, Malaysia, the Philippines, Singapore, and Thailand.

9. The East Asia Economic Caucus, a proposed free trade zone, is to encompass the countries of the Association of Southeast Asian Nations (ASEAN) plus China, South Korea, and Japan.

10. The Cooperation Council for the Arab States of the Gulf, begun in 1981, consists of Bahrain, Kuwait, Oman, Qatar, Saudi Arabia and the United Arab Emirates. This common market has been proposed for 2007.

11. The African Economic Community (AEC) is to unite the African continent. Signed in 1991 by fifty-one countries, the Treaty Establishing the African Economic Community calls for the establishment of a Pan-African Economic and Monetary Union, a single market, and a Pan-African Parliament within thirty-four years from the date of its signing.[31]

Unity is the way of the future. The West shall recognize that AmEuropean unity is a great step forward for mankind, a great step toward greater individual liberty, personal freedom, open-mindedness, tolerance, and justice, all preconditions for world peace. For this purpose, AmEuropeans—the citizens of AmEuropa—shall unite in peace, freedom, and democracy. To this end, the countries of the United States of America, Canada and twenty-five of the twenty-seven member states of the European Union shall establish the Alliance of AmEuropa.

Chapter 2
Will Unity Come Too Late?

"… It has already happened once before in history," wrote renowned Spanish philosopher Ortega y Gasset, "that a great civilization has died through not being able to adopt a substitute for its traditional idea of the state."[32] In *Civilization on Trial,* Toynbee attributes the fall of Greek civilization to the Greeks failure to unify.

"And the peculiar interest of Graeco-Roman history for us lies in the fact that the Greek civilization broke down in the fifth century B.C. through failing to find a successful response to the very challenge which is confronting our own Western civilization in our own lifetime. …And this political failure was the cause of its break-down…. So long as the economic life of each city-state remained parochial, they could all still afford to be parochial in their political life as well. The parochial sovereignty of each city-state, vis-à-vis every other, might and did breed perpetual petty wars, yet, in the economic circumstances of the age, these wars were not deadly in their social effects. But the new economic system, introduced by the Attic economic revolution under the spur of the stoppage of Greek colonial expansion, was based on local production for international exchange. It could only work successfully if, on the economic plane, the city-states gave up their parochialism and became interdependent. And a system of international economic interdependence could only be made to work if it could be brought within the framework of a system of international political interdependence: some international system of political law and order which would place a restraint upon the anarchic parochial sovereignty of the local city-states.... The Roman Empire—which was really an international league for Greek and other, culturally related, city-states—may be regarded as a tardy solution of the problem.... But the epitaph of the Roman Empire is 'too late'.... The *Pax Romana* [Roman Peace] was a peace of exhaustion, a peace which was not creative and therefore not permanent. It was a peace and order that came four centuries after its due time."[33]

Will the West commit the same blunder of not unifying due to complacency, indolence, disorder, and the lack of creativity? Or will the West wake up and take action in time before it is, as it was for the Greco-Roman society, "too late"?

"The history of the last 5,000 years" Toynbee explains, "seems to show that, in the Age of Civilization, the question at issue is not whether a fractured political configuration of society or a unitary one is preferable. A fractured configuration is bound to be ephemeral; so the practical question is: At what stage and by what means is political unity going to be brought about?"[34] In the Age of Amity of the twenty-first century, the loose political unity of AmEuropa shall be the "preferable unitary political configuration" for the survival of Western civilization.

"The first lesson in history is modesty," wrote Will and Ariel Durant in *The Lessons of History*.[35] In addition, the Bible warns, "Pride goes before destruction, and haughtiness (a haughty spirit) before a fall." (Proverbs 16:18) Hence, to those either arrogant or ignorant enough to defy the laws of life by believing that one nation-state can forever remain the sole superpower, I say to thee, study the rise and fall of great powers and remember that change is a law of life and nature. America's share of the world economy has long been in steady decline since the end of World War II. "The U.S.," Nobel laureate Robert Mundell says, "has gone from being the biggest creditor nation to being the biggest debtor nation by far."[36] As America's share of the global economy declines, so too will its influence in the world. As the European Union grows in size, so too will its share of the global economy and its influence. Moreover, the U.S. dollar continues to fall, whereas the euro continues to rise: on January 18, 2002, €1 euro equaled $0.88 U.S. cents; on January 10, 2007, €1 euro equaled $1.34 U.S. dollars. Let it not be forgotten: North America needs Europe just as Europe needs North America. As the two pillars of the West, they complement each other in AmEuropa.

World peace can never be achieved as long as the divisive-mindedness of Western nationalism exists. For world peace to be achieved, AmEuropean unity is a pre-condition. Moreover, an incessant indifference or refusal to unite would constitute the demise of the West.

The fortitude and solidarity of AmEuropean unity shall bequeath upon all AmEuropeans—regardless of race, creed, color, sexual orientation, or class—greater individual liberty and personal freedom as well as increased prosperity, security, stability, and peace.

Chapter 3
AmEuropean Unity

AmEuropean unity is the unity of North America and Europe, the core of the West, which includes the Atlantic alliance (NATO). AmEuropean unity is to be achieved progressively, democratically, and voluntarily through the creation of the Alliance of AmEuropa.

AmEuropa can be seen as a deepening friendship, partnership, and cooperation of NATO. AmEuropean unity begins with a belief in the commonality, concord, and unity of AmEuropean nations in AmEuropa, the Atlantic alliance, and Western civilization.

AmEuropean unity advances cooperation among peoples and most importantly endows the individual with the right to free movement within a vast area of freedom that stretches from western California, British Columbia, and Alaska to eastern Finland, Poland, and Hungary.

Central to AmEuropean unity is the reinstatement of the freedom of movement of citizens between North America and Europe, similar to the freedom of movement that existed during much of the cosmopolitan seventeenth and eighteenth centuries as well as a part of the nineteenth century. During much of these centuries, people could circulate freely between Europe and North America. "Britain did not require of foreigners that they provide themselves with passports in order to disembark their shores," writes Martin Lloyd in *The Passport: The History of Man's Most Travelled Document.*[37] "A colonist," he adds, "desirous of leaving Virginia in the seventeenth century had to apply to the governor for a passport and this application was examined and approved by the council and general court of the colony. A pass was only issued after verification that the traveller had posted a notice of his intended voyage on the church door for two Sundays and had settled all his debts."[38] So simple were the requirements.

AmEuropean reintegration helps to broaden the horizons of AmEuropeans and helps to eliminate any prejudices and fear AmEuropeans might have of other AmEuropean cultures.

AmEuropean unity strengthens the Atlantic alliance and facilitates the integration of its peoples and economies to ensure the cooperation and partnership of its governments, thereby alleviating disputes that could possibly lead to trade wars and conflicts, both hot and cold. Furthermore, AmEuropean unity extends the liberties and freedoms of all AmEuropeans.

Only AmEuropean unity can save the West from further decline and prevent its fall. The decline of the West, first documented scientifically by legendary historian Oswald Spengler, has long been underway.[39] If the West continues to decline and divide itself, then the fall of the West is imminent.

Many wonder where all the current chaos in the world is leading us to. It is leading us to AmEuropean unity, the creation of the Alliance of AmEuropa. Just as the hatred and destruction of the Second World War resulted in European unity, the hatred and destruction against the West shall result in AmEuropean unity. The enemies of the West shall galvanize the solidarity of the West bringing forth AmEuropean unity and the creation of AmEuropa.

The West has long been without a vision of a better future for its peoples, without a sense of purpose, and a sense of being. This lack of vision, sense of purpose, and sense of being has created frustration, boredom, and even despair among the people of the West. A common goal has been missing since the fall of the Soviet Union. The people of the West need a vision, a grand goal, something to look forward to, something to work for, something to unite for, something great to achieve.

AmEuropean unity is the path that leads AmEuropeans out of their boredom, bewilderment, and frustration. AmEuropa gives AmEuropeans a vision of what their future will look like and a grand goal to achieve; it gives AmEuropeans something to look forward to, something to create, something to work for, something to unite for, something great to achieve.

In support of unity and the rejection of nationalism, Ortega y Gasset wrote:

> "The European cannot live unless embarked upon some great unifying enterprise. When this is lacking, he becomes degraded, grows slack, his soul is paralyzed. We have a commencement of this before our eyes. The groups which up to to-day have been known as nations arrived about a century ago at their highest point of expansion. Nothing more can be done with them except lead

them to a higher evolution. They are now mere past accumulating all around Europe, weighing it down, imprisoning it. With more vital freedom than ever, we feel that we cannot breath the air within our nations, because it is a confined air. What was before a nation open to all the minds of heaven, has turned into something provincial, an enclosed space."[40]

If the predominantly Latin Italians, Spaniards, and Portuguese can live and work side by side with the predominantly Germanic Anglo-Saxons, Germans, and Scandinavians, then Americans can live and work side by side with Britons and Europeans, for the cultural and linguistic difference between a Spaniard and a German is greater than between an American and a German. In fact, according to the U.S. Census 2000, the largest ethnic group in America, counting 42.8 million Americans or 15.2% of the population, is German. The second largest is Irish with 30.5 million or 10.8% of the population.[41] In Germany, many Germans proudly say that almost every German family has had at least one family member immigrate to America or Canada at sometime or another.

Already in 1930, Ortega y Gasset wrote, "I say, then, that to-day the average Italian, Spaniard, or German is less differentiated in vital tone from the North American or Argentine then he was thirty years ago. And this is a fact the people of America ought not to forget."[42] Today, with the rapid means of communication and transportation the difference is significantly less. In light of this, most Americans, Europeans, and Canadians, having been raised in the West, share common languages, religions, technologies, values, virtues, and beliefs in democracy, equality, liberty, freedom, and human rights as well as a common way of life, a common literature, a common past, and a common future. This cultural bond is important in creating a common feeling, a common cause, a core of unity for world peace, a nucleus for democracy, freedom, and liberty in a world that is in need of law and order, prosperity, security, stability, and peace.

In the West, the divisive ideology of nationalism is a way of the past, a way of the nineteenth and twentieth centuries. The formation of multinational alliances, organizations, and unions, for the purpose of free trade and the free movement of citizens, is the way of the future, the way of the twenty-first century in the Age of Amity. "Nationalism's recent gains," wrote Toynbee "cannot compare with the gains that the unifying movement has been making in the course of these last five millennia; and in the Atomic Age ... mankind has to choose between political reunification and mass-suicide."[43]

Article V of the North Atlantic Treaty states, *"The Parties agree that an armed attack against one or more of them in Europe or North America shall be considered an attack against them all."*[44] Hence, if the nations of the Atlantic alliance (NATO) are willing to die for each other in war, then they should be allowed to live and work with each other in peace. Nonetheless, for the Alliance to succeed politically, economically, and culturally, member countries of AmEuropa must meet certain political, economic, and cultural requirements. Let it be clear that cultural does not mean racial. For the free movement of citizens to succeed without cultural anxiety and tension at the outset of forming AmEuropa, all member countries should have a Western cultural tradition regardless of their race, creed, or color. Other nations, however, could join the Alliance at a later time if they wish to and if the other member nations agree upon their accession. For economic and political requirements, see chapter 10 entitled "Alliance Member Countries and Proposed Accession Requirements."

Chapter 4
AmEuropa, The Next Superpower—Keeping Ahead of China

What will be the next superpower—the EU, China, India, or AmEuropa? The answer depends on whether the West has the motivation, power, and will to remain a world leader. Although some books claim the EU to already be an economic superpower and to be "the next superpower," a great many people claim China to be the next superpower. These people say China simply because they have never heard of AmEuropa.

Since the second Iraq war, many European politicians feel the need to build a superpower to act as a "counterweight" to American supremacy and American unilateralism. "We are building a new world superpower. The European Union is about the projection of collective power, wealth, and influence. That collective strength makes individual nations more powerful—and it will make the EU as a whole a global power," British Prime Minister Tony Blair told journalist and author T.R. Reid when speaking of the EU.[45] The European Union has recently emerged as an economic, cultural, and political superpower alongside the United States. China, on the other hand, needs approximately two decades to catch up, giving the West a little time to create the Alliance of AmEuropa before it is "too late." "China's GDP," Ambassador Schnabel writes, "could be as large as America's by the year 2020."[46]

Economically, the EU's GDP equals that of the United States: the EU's 2006 estimated purchasing power parity GDP is $12.82 trillion compared to the U.S.'s $12.98 trillion, and the EU's official exchange rate GDP is $13.62 trillion versus the U.S.'s $13.22 trillion. China's purchasing power parity GDP is already $10 trillion, but its official exchange rate GDP is still a mere $2.512 trillion.[47] Culturally, the U.S. and EU's consumer products, entertainment, and arts are bought the world over. China's arts and entertainment have yet to reach a similar status. Only China's consumer products are bought the world over. Having an economy as large as America's, a greater number of votes than the U.S. in world organizations, and sending "ten times as many soldiers than the United States to peacekeeping missions in Africa, Central Asia, even Central America," and providing larger amounts of both development assistance and humanitarian aid than the U.S., plus the strength of the euro, give the European Union new political and economic clout and influence in the world that elevate it to the status of a new superpower in terms of soft power.[48] Soft power is the cultural, economic and political power to influence other countries without the use of a military force to coerce; hard power, on the other hand, is military might. Since "hard power is so costly to maintain" and generates "hatred from those who are weaker," many Europeans believe "soft power amounts to greater power. The Oxford historian

John Pinder makes this point: 'Too much American hegemony is dangerous for the Americans as well as for others. The burden is too great for one country to carry alone.'[49] The combination of Europe's soft power and America's hard power makes for the perfect alliance and mega superpower of two superpowers.

Many political analysts perceive the rise of China as a threat. In an essay entitled "China: The Challenge of a Rising Power," Ross Munro, the director of Asian Studies at the Center for Security Studies in Washington, D.C., writes, "Virtually every serious strategist thinker in the Untied States today agrees that China, if current trends continue, represents a greater potential danger in the long term than any other nation in the world…. No issue in U.S.-China relations today is more volatile, or more charged with immediate danger for the United States, than Taiwan."[50] "China presents a long-term danger…," writes Francis Fukuyama in *America at the Crossroads.*[51] Furthermore, Samuel Huntington writes, "…The rise of China and the increasing assertiveness of this 'biggest player in the history of man' will place tremendous stress on international stability in the early twenty-first century. The emergence of China as the dominant power in East and Southeast Asia would be contrary to American interests…."[52] In light of the serious danger of a rising China, Fukuyama points out that "neoconservatives" such as "Kristol and Kagan … called for regime change … for China, which in the period before September 11 constituted their central opponent in the international system."[53] For the year 2007, China increased its annual military budget by 17.8 percent. Furthermore, China has over eight hundred rockets aimed at Taiwan.

Neither the United States alone nor the European Union alone—each working in its own interest, thereby sometimes putting the two at odds with one another—will be able to remain the world's leading superpower for long after the emergence of China and eventually India as superpowers in the near future. Through the creation of AmEuropa as the next superpower, the West can remain a world leader for a half millennium. AmEuropa shall keep the West a step ahead of China and its Chinese Communist Party, a repressive authoritarian government with a poor record in human rights, from taking the lead in world affairs as the next superpower.

China has a major advantage in that it is already unified. As China's massive population of over 1.3 billion will still outnumber AmEuropa's population of approximately 818 million, it is imperative that the nations of the West learn to overcome their cultural, political, and social differences and unite or forever relinquish leadership to China and a potential coalition of enemies. An Asian-Islamic coalition would tower over the West like a giant over a dwarf. In fact, an Asian-Islamic coalition appeared at the U.N. World Conference on Human Rights in Vienna in 1993 to defeat the human rights supporters of the West.[54] Unfortunately, a large part of the world still does not live in a free society. According to the Freedom House's 2005 comparative assessment, eighty-nine countries or 44% of the world's population are considered free. Fifty-four countries or 19% of the world's population are considered partly free: their basic political rights and civil liberties are limited. And forty-nine countries or 37% of the world's population are considered not free: their basic political rights and civil liberties are denied.[55]

Instead of keeping ahead of China, those in the West with a defeatist attitude passively go along with the idea of China becoming the next superpower. Do these people comprehend what kind of example the current Chinese government would set if it were to lead as the next superpower? Has the West forgotten that the Chinese government is communist, commits serious human rights abuses, denies internationally recognized worker rights, imposes a coercive birth limitation policy, and suppresses religious freedom? [56]

If the West does nothing out of apathy and laziness to stay ahead of China, the repressive, authoritarian Chinese Communist Party will soon become the leader in world affairs. An incessant failure to unite would constitute the demise of the West. If the West could win the Cold War against such a formidable opponent as the Soviet Union through unity, then the West can win the war against terrorism and stay ahead of China through AmEuropean unity.

The West's concentration of collective power shall be found in AmEuropa. Since most all member countries of NATO shall also be member countries of AmEuropa, NATO is to be the military organization of AmEuropa responsible for the defense of all member countries of AmEuropa. Consequently, AmEuropa is to become the nucleus of any economic and political unification on a global scale. Americans, Europeans, and Canadians, however, must unite economically and to some extent politically before world peace becomes feasible. The unity of the West in AmEuropa is a prerequisite for solidarity on a global scale and world peace. AmEuropa, a world-unifier, is a beacon of light for the West and the world, beckoning us to a new world of unity, love, peace, and a better quality of life.

AmEuropa is a new kind of superpower, a superpower built on the strength of voluntary, democratic unity and not by coercion or oppression. AmEuropa is without imperialistic claims, unlike China, which has revealed its desire to take in free Taiwan someday. In sum, AmEuropa is a superpower built in peace, through peace, for peace and the extension of individual liberty and personal freedom.

Chapter 5
How to Prevent the Downfall of the West and the End of Western Culture

Some historians, political analysts, politicians, and writers—such as Spengler in *Decline of the West,* Buchanan in *The Death of the West,* Barzun in *Dawn to Decadence,* and Kagan in *Of Paradise and Power*—have declared respectively the decline of the West, the death of the West, the end of Western culture, and "the West" per se to be passé.[57] Barzun in *Dawn to Decadence* claims that Western culture is ending. "… In the West," Barzun writes, "the culture of the last 500 years is ending…."[58] By "Decadence," he means a "falling off." "It doesn't [end], of course, in the literal sense of stoppage of total ruin…. The loss it faces is that of Possibility. The forms of art as of life seem exhausted, the stages of development have been run through. Institutions function painfully. Repetition and frustration are the intolerable result. Boredom and fatigue are great historical forces."[59]

The end of Western culture and civilization must not be if the West can revive itself through harmony, creativity, self-determination, unity, and peace. It must be the elements of decline and decadence, such as arrogance, boredom, laziness, divisive-mindedness, and war, that "fall off" and not the culture and civilization of the West. The West must retain the free will to self-determine its own future. "The futures of the United States and the West," writes Huntington, "depend upon Americans reaffirming their commitment to Western civilization."[60]

To revitalize the West, I have set a goal for the West to achieve, a "Possibility," one that brings the West together in a joint venture for the attainment of a common good, a common homeland in AmEuropa. The exciting path of joint venture to AmEuropean unity as well as the greater peace, individual liberty, and personal freedom resulting therefrom do away with the "intolerable repetition, frustration, boredom, and fatigue" that is bringing the West to an end. Joint venture stimulates creativity. The arts and sciences, commerce and technology, and the individual all stand to gain from this AmEuropean joint venture.

"A culture," wrote Toynbee, "can expand only at the expense of other cultures."[61] Hence, the West's influence in the world can either expand or recede, for nothing remains the same: change is a law of life and nature. If North America significantly limits immigration from Europe and if Europe significantly limits immigration from North America, two separate and distinct civilizations will emerge, thereby ending Western civilization. North America cannot reject its Western heritage: to do so is to make the same mistake as Nazi Germany did. "...The Germans," wrote Toynbee, "had played a leading part in the development of Western Civilization. Martin Luther was a German; modern Western music is a German art. Yet the Nazi rejected Germany's Western heritage and jettisoned it."[62] We are living in a time when the strength of AmEuropean unity and the creative cultural exchange facilitated by AmEuropean integration are urgent.

"…Levels of Civilization," Samuel Huntington writes, "may simply reflect phases in the evolution of civilizations…. As the competition among its constituent elements tapers off and a universal state emerges, the civilization reaches its highest level of Civilization, its 'golden age,' with a flowering of morality, art, literature, philosophy, technology, and martial, economic, and political competence."[63] AmEuropa is this "universal state" in which competition has tapered off and Western civilization reaches its "golden age."

Americans, Canadians, and Europeans once enjoyed the freedom of living and working in each other's sovereign nations. Unfortunately, the rise of nationalism in the nineteenth century stripped the nations of the West of that right. Today, due to the high level of migration from underdeveloped countries to industrialized countries coupled with the constant threat of terrorism, Western governments have imposed extremely stringent immigration laws that deprive the citizens of America, Canada, and Europe of their earlier freedom to live and work in each other's countries. By limiting the movement of citizens between North America and Europe, the parts, the nations of North America, will begin to "fall off" from the whole, Western civilization. If allowed to continue over a long period of time, North American nations will develop a cultural identity separate from other Western countries, thus eventually creating two distinct civilizations: a North American civilization and a European civilization.

It is negative and destructive to dwell upon any differences we might have. To create harmony and the Kantian notion of "perpetual peace,"[64] we must highlight our commonalities and study our common heritage in a common civilization, which originated from the Greco-Roman civilization, was born in the period of Charlemagne and the Carolingian renaissance, passed through the Middle Ages, the Reformation, the Renaissance, and the Enlightenment periods to present-day culture, science, and technology.

The West does have another option to the defeatist attitude practiced by many of its citizens who claim that China will be the next superpower. Through AmEuropean unity and the creation of AmEuropa, the West shall have the opportunity to peacefully stay ahead of China as the next superpower and world leader.

Will the West seize this opportunity of strength, liberty, freedom, peace, and prosperity in and through AmEuropean unity or will it continue to linger and decline due to apathy, indifference, laziness, and defeatism? As the adage says, "Unity is strength!"

Deriving his emphatic declaration from the bible (Matthew 12:25)—which states *"Jesus knew their thoughts, and said to them, 'Every kingdom divided against itself will be ruined, and every city or house divided against itself will not stand'"*—U.S. President Abraham Lincoln, in his Republican nomination acceptance speech for the Senate in 1858, declared: "A house divided against itself cannot stand." Hence, in the same way, the West divided against itself will not stand. Any further division and denial of the West only ensures its decline and fall.

Some Americans complain about the French by saying that they are ungrateful, for "we bailed them out" of two world wars. The French, however, could say the same, that we are ungrateful, for they bailed us out during the American Revolution and gave us the Statue of Liberty. Without French assistance during the American Revolution, an American victory would have been unlikely and the American revolutionaries would have been hung as revolutionary criminal insurgents. The French supplied the American revolutionaries with arms to fight the British, and the French fleet blocked the British army from the sea. The reader familiar with French literature might recall Beaumarchais, the eighteenth-century playwright of the Barber of Seville and the Marriage of Figaro, who went into debt purchasing arms for the American revolutionaries. In 1885, France presented America with a statue of Liberty Enlightening the World, more commonly known as the Statue of Liberty, to commemorate the centennial of the United States and as a gesture of friendship between America and France. Furthermore, some Americans who support American political and military unilateralism as the global "hyperpower"[65] and who are upset at French reluctance to support the second Iraq war by placing bumper stickers on their cars saying "Boycott France" or by calling French fries "freedom fries" are sowing discord among partners and are contributing to the alienation of the United States. Disrespect cultivates disrespect; discord cultivates discord. Similarly, European politicians wishing to create a European superpower as a "counterweight" to American power also sow discord. Unfortunately for Americans and Europeans alike, the sowing of discord on both sides of the Atlantic further widens the gap between America and Europe that if allowed to continue will inevitably lead to trade wars and possibly other conflicts (perhaps hot, perhaps cold) and divide the West. Because of this widening gap, Francois Heisbourg, president of the International Institute for Strategic Studies, poses the question: *"La fin de l'Occident?" (The End of the West?)*[66] America and Europe have always needed each other and will always need each other; to think otherwise is arrogance or ignorance or both or perhaps a form of jealousy or hatred.

For the safety and security of the people of both the West and the world, all forms of alienation and discord must be reversed. The enemies of the West must learn that they cannot stir up discord between America and Europe and cannot play one against the other. Discord leads to division, causing weakness, instability, and eventually destruction and death. In other words, division renders the West less secure and the world more dangerous. Unity renders the West more secure and the world safer.

For the good of America and Americans, the U.S. cannot alienate or isolate itself from its European and Canadian partners in an interconnected global economy in which the EU and Canada are America's strongest trading partners.[67] According to the White House, "The United States and the European Union are each other's largest sources of foreign direct investment, with the 2002 stock of U.S. direct investment in the European Union reaching $700 billion and EU investment in the United States reaching $850 billion."[68] "For the year 2000," Reid writes, "Europeans provided more than 65 percent of all foreign investment in the United States."[69] And according to the German newspaper Der Tagesspiegel, the volume of Import-Export transactions between the EU and the U.S. amounted to approximately €1.25 billion euros daily in 2005.[70]

AmEuropa
The Future of The West and The Next Superpower

Given that the threat of the Soviet Union has ended, does not mean we have to gradually revert back to creating old Western rivalries that so often lead to antagonism, dissension, trade wars, and conflict. The emergence of a bi- or multi-polar West will create tension, trade wars, alienation, dissension, and eventually new rivalries and conflicts by which the West had long been plagued throughout history. Whenever two or more superpowers have existed simultaneously in the world, alienation, antagonism, rivalry, and eventually war—either hot or cold—most often emerged between them. Since the collapse of the Soviet Union, however, other enemies of the West have been emerging, forcing the West to confront new enemies. To ensure "perpetual peace" the West must first eliminate any possibility of discord among its members. The way to prevent any possible discord between two Western superpowers is to integrate the peoples and economies of the two superpowers by creating one Alliance, one AmEuropa, and one AmEuropean citizenship while keeping national citizenships and regional cultural identities.

The integration of our peoples fosters intergovernmental cooperation, partnership, teamwork and the rejuvenation of the West. The strength afforded by AmEuropean unity in the Alliance of AmEuropa ensures for a long time to come that powers like China, North Korea, Iran, and the Islamic extremists as well as India and Russia will not surpass the West in terms of political and cultural influence, economic strength, and military power.

If the West—out of apathy, laziness, lack of creativity, or lack of will—fails to create the Alliance of AmEuropa, the demise of the West shall be a forgone conclusion.

AmEuropa is the last chance for the West to save itself from further decline and fall. AmEuropa is the worldly savior of the West.

Chapter 6
The AmEuropean Greater Common Market and the AmEuropean Area of Freedom

The AmEuropean Greater Common Market (AGCM) is the great single domestic market in which most internal trade barriers such as quotas and tariffs are to be abolished between member countries of AmEuropa. The AmEuropean Area of Freedom (AAF), more or less corresponding to the AGCM, is the area in which the AmEuropean four freedoms—the free movement of goods, capital, services, and citizens while retaining border controls where desired—are to be permitted and encouraged by law. Furthermore, the AmEuropean Area of Freedom, which includes all Alliance member countries, is the area in which all AmEuropeans shall have the right to live and work.

The AmEuropean Greater Common Market and the AmEuropean Area of Freedom show good faith among member nations. This good faith among partners creates solidarity. In addition, as a larger cultural, economic and political block, AmEuropa affords individual nation-states the ability to greater influence the cultural, economic and political future of Western civilization and the world.

The AmEuropean Greater Common Market and the AmEuropean Area of Freedom shall increase foreign investment and open up markets in Europe to American and Canadian businesses as well as afford American and Canadian citizens the opportunity to work for British and European employers in Europe. Likewise, the AmEuropean Greater Common Market and the AmEuropean Area of Freedom shall increase foreign investment and open up markets in America and Canada to British and European businesses as well as afford British and European citizens the opportunity to work for American and Canadian employers in the U.S. and Canada.

By permitting the free movement of goods, services, capital, and citizens, the much-needed foreign investment shall be able to cross the Atlantic more easily and in greater abundance. Hence, the AmEuropean Greater Common Market coupled with the AmEuropean Area of Freedom shall spur economic growth. AmEuropa is economically a win-win situation for not only Alliance member countries but also developing countries. The TransAtlantic Business Dialogue (TABD) November 2006 Submission of the U.S.–EU Economic Ministerial Meeting states:

> "...We cannot afford to ignore the benefits of further transatlantic liberalization of product, service and investment markets. The mutual benefits arising from such a process would amount to *increases of European and US GDP of up to 3%,* as calculated by the OECD in 2005.

Moreover, the benefits of further transatlantic liberalization would extend to third countries, in particular developing countries, who would gain access to a consolidated transatlantic market of some 700 million consumers. Were the US and EU to move closer towards a single transatlantic market, with common and streamlined regulatory procedures and standards, developing countries would be major beneficiaries."[71]

Protectionism, limiting trade between America, Canada, and Europe, hinders growth. Likewise, restricted movement of Americans, Canadians, and Europeans limits economic growth, employment opportunities, individual liberty, personal freedom, and the personal exchange of constructive ideas. U.S. President Benjamin Harrison's McKinley Tariff, a protective tariff, not only made consumer prices soar at home but also damaged American exports abroad. By raising the price of imports, the McKinley Tariff denied foreign competition. Foreign competition, however, keeps consumer prices down. Furthermore, since America raised the tariffs on foreign imports, foreign countries retaliated by raising tariffs on American goods. Moreover, President Herbert Hoover's Smoot-Hawley Tariff made the depression of the 1930s worse then it should have been. [72] As a result, most U.S. presidents and other world leaders have since supported free trade. "For example," according to the encyclopedia Wikipedia, " theorists of Chinese nationalism within the People's Republic of China have articulated the idea that China's national power is substantially enhanced, rather than being reduced, by engaging in international trade and multinational organizations."[73] Prosperity grows with trade and foreign investment. "… Americans," Reid writes, "are more aware than they were fifteen years ago that it is beneficial for any nation—and particularly a country with a massive balance of trade deficit—to take in foreign investment. Maybe Americans now realize that the money pouring in is creating factories and stores and jobs." [74] Accordingly, TransAtlantic Business Dialogue (TABD) U.S. Chairman Charles Prince of Citicorp and EU Chairman Martin Broughton of British Airways have made a plea to end "economic nationalism and protectionist sentiment." In their "Report and Recommendations to the 2006 US-EU Summit Leaders," they wrote:

> …30 Chairmen and CEOs participating in the TABD are seriously concerned about the rise of economic nationalism and protectionist sentiment in both Member States of the European Union and the United States. Our economies prosper when they are open to foreign investment and capital, and when people and goods can travel freely as possible across national borders. We must not jeopardize the important progress we have achieved in the past in removing barriers to trade and investment by erecting new ones for short-term political gain. [75]

The AmEuropean Greater Common Market coupled with the AmEuropean Area of Freedom shall stimulate creative thinking by facilitating the exchange of ideas through the free movement of citizens. The personal, face-to-face exchange of new ideas between the diverse peoples of the twenty-seven member nations of AmEuropa will be creatively and intellectually stimulating of unprecedented proportions, thus inspiring AmEuropeans with innovative ideas in architecture, the arts and sciences, and technology.

The AmEuropean Greater Common Market coupled with the AmEuropean Area of Freedom shall lower unemployment and help reduce outsourcing to cheaper labor markets outside of AmEuropa. America, Canada, and Europe shall be able to freely and legally take advantage of each other's labor market as a pool to fill their labor needs, thereby according both continents unprecedented labor and employment opportunities. Expanding businesses on both side of the Atlantic reduces unemployment, for these expanding businesses will need to hire local labor. Furthermore, the AmEuropean Greater Common Market and the AmEuropean Area of Freedom eliminate much of the fear factor of hardship by eliminating much of the bureaucratic red tape hitherto required of North American and European businesses to access new clients and open up new markets on each other's continent. The Greater AmEuropean Common Market and the AmEuropean Area of Freedom shall give both North American and European companies unprecedented freedom in finding qualified workers; in the same way, both North American and European workers shall have unprecedented freedom in choosing an employer. Furthermore, the AmEuropean Area of Freedom shall allow companies to transfer employees freely from one AmEuropean city or country to another with great ease, thereby helping to keep current company employees employed. Furthermore, in addition to the lower wage-earning workers that have immigrated to the West in the past, the NATO alliance member nations of Eastern Europe shall be able to provide AmEuropean companies with sufficient affordable and well-educated labor in the future that AmEuropean companies shall no longer feel pressed to leave the nations of AmEuropa in order to survive. Since joining the European Union, Spain's unemployment has declined dramatically.

As it is illegal for Americans and Canadians (without the required official documents) to live and work in Europe and for Britons and Europeans to live and work in America and Canada, most Americans and Canadians cannot consider working in Great Britain and Europe and most Britons and Europeans cannot consider working in America and Canada. Most people simply allow themselves to be caged in physically, culturally, economically, and politically: physically by remaining in their native nation-state, culturally by not choosing a culture with mores and a lifestyle more to their liking, economically by not taking the opportunity to expand their work and job opportunities elsewhere where there is work, and politically by not choosing a nation-state that better fits their political ideology where they would live a happier life in a system more to their liking among politically likeminded people.

The point of the AmEuropean Area of Freedom is not to remove border controls in order to allow anyone to pass, but rather to permit AmEuropeans—the citizens of AmEuropa—to live and work in any member country. Hence, the freedom of movement granted by the AmEuropean Area of Freedom is a right for AmEuropeans to live and work anywhere in AmEuropa but not a right to pass national borders unchecked.

Corporations, businesses, and individuals all stand to gain from AmEuropa. As not all countries have the same job markets, those who cannot find jobs at home can find them in any of the other twenty-six member countries. Some professions are more in demand in some countries than other countries. Why deprive ourselves of a peaceful, beneficial freedom that helps to improve the quality of life? AmEuropa does something to help.

Many AmEuropean families, friends, and loved ones have been separated due to the ever-stringent immigration laws. In the 1990s, I remember watching a British lady on TV tell the media that she could not enter the U.S. at the end of her flight because she did not have a so-called fiancé visa even though Britons (like most Western Europeans) are permitted to enter the U.S. as tourists for a period of up to three months. The problem arose when the immigration office asked the purpose of her stay. She replied that she was going to visit her fiancé. That is when the immigration officer asked to see her "fiancé visa," for he no longer considered her a tourist. She then had to return to Britain. With the Alliance of AmEuropa, such embarrassing situations between America and Britain could no longer happen, especially when you think that America was formerly a British colony.

The AmEuropean Area of Freedom shall return a freedom to the citizens of North America and Europe that was taken away long ago. In much of the seventeenth, eighteenth, and even nineteenth centuries, people could circulate freely between Europe and North America. The AmEuropean Area of Freedom shall reinstate this freedom of movement between North America and Europe while keeping border controls. This freedom will make the hateful hearts of the enemies of the West envious, for they would prefer to see Westerners loose freedom rather than gain freedom.

As nature has a mysterious way of bringing success to active and optimistic team players and failure to complacent and pessimistic egotists, the future of the world will hold up those nations who have learned concordance and work cooperatively in accord with other nations as team players and hold down those nations who alienate other nations, reject concordance, and work egotistically and divisively against other nations.

For those Americans who fear too much immigration from Canada or Europe or vice versa, from America and Canada to Europe, must not fear, for the implementation of Europe's Schengen Agreement with its free movement of persons without border controls shows that people of affluent countries seldom emigrate from their homeland. In the European Union, migration is predominantly from new Europe (the newer EU member states of Eastern Europe) to old Europe (the older EU member states of Western Europe) and not within old Europe. Migration in old Europe is primarily short term for cultural interests, job development, or linguistic improvement. Moreover, immigrants from countries with commensurate economies and social security and welfare systems do not threaten the economy and welfare state of the host country, for they have no need to immigrate in order to take advantage of the wealthier country's economy and welfare system. As Europeans have a high standard of living and a superior welfare system, America would not see an overwhelming large influx of European immigrants to the United States with the inception of the AmEuropean Area of Freedom; and the EU can be rest assured that it would not be overrun by Americans trying to take advantage of its welfare system, as America's unemployment rate is at a low 4.5 percent (December

2006). At any rate, immigrants from countries of the same civilization as the host country do not threaten the cultural identity and language of the host country, for these immigrants can assimilate easily; their cultural groups and linguistic families are related.

Each nation-state shall have the right to determine the duration of residency and the amount of payment into the new welfare system required before a new AmEuropean arrival to a different Alliance member country can enter the host country's welfare system. This will prevent any abuses of another member country's welfare system.

Seeing that Congress approved the construction of a seven hundred-mile wall along the U.S.–Mexico border, the U.S. with its low level of unemployment shall be able to benefit economically from the highly skilled yet inexpensive labor force from Eastern Europe. A part of the many polish workers that migrated to Great Britain in 2006 would have had the option of continuing on to Canada and America if AmEuropa had already been in place.

How does the AmEuropean free movement of citizens work? When an AmEuropean citizen decides to take up residency in another Alliance member country, then he or she shall register with the local office of the U.S. Citizenship and Immigration Services (USCIS), a part of the U.S. Department of Homeland Security (DHS), in the U.S. or, depending on the member country, with the foreign registry or foreign police authorities responsible for immigration services. Registering with the local authorities is a mere bureaucratic formality to keep law and order as well as statistics. AmEuropeans shall no longer be denied residency, thereby affording all AmEuropean citizens—regardless of race, creed, color, sexual orientation, or class—the right to residency anywhere within AmEuropa. That is equality, a hitherto unprecedented equality.

By not charging AmEuropeans duties for their goods or trade when crossing internal national borders within AmEuropa, border control guards shall be able to concentrate on looking for harmful, illegal contraband and terrorists, thereby reducing cross border crime and terrorism. Furthermore, AmEuropeans shall no longer be required to travel across town to pick up a package from a postal customs office requiring the payment of an import tax of 22% (depending on the country) for a product (whatever its size) sent from North America to Europe or from Europe to North America.

Each nation-state shall retain the right to determine its own immigration policy from non-Alliance member countries. New immigrants from non-Alliance member countries, who are not citizens of any member country of AmEuropa, should not be granted the right to free movement within the Alliance, as that is a right afforded to those holding AmEuropean citizenship, that is to say citizenship of a member country of AmEuropa.

American citizens preferring to live and work in a Canadian or European welfare state shall be permitted to do so. Canadians and Europeans who prefer the American style of free-market economy to their own shall be permitted to live and work in America. The AmEuropean Greater Common Market and the AmEuropean Area of Freedom shall make it easier not only for businesses, both small and large, to expand into new markets and to hire and transfer employees but also for citizens to find employment, develop their professional skills, and broaden their horizons. AmEuropa is a win-win situation for both businesses and individuals on both sides of the Atlantic.

Chapter 7
AmEuropean Cosmopolitanism

"…Nationalism," wrote Toynbee, "is a recrudescence of the worship of collective human power from which the higher religions have been seeking to liberate mankind…. In the Atomic Age, Nationalism is a death wish…. The wish for reunification is a wish for life and good. …A voluntary renunciation of national sovereignty is the only condition on which the nations can survive. It is not unreasonable to hope that mankind will be reasonable to this extent." [76] In 1886, having more or less experienced the rise of nationalism in Europe, Nietzsche wrote of "the insanity of nationality" inducing "pathological estrangement" and that "shortsighted and quick-handed politicians who are at the top today with the help of this insanity" have no "inkling that their separatist policies can of necessity only be *entr'acte* [interlude] policies."[77] The rise of nationalism in the nineteenth century brought about the decline of cosmopolitanism. Nevertheless, with the advent of European unity, Europe has been experiencing a renaissance in European cosmopolitanism.

Webster's New Universal Unabridged Dictionary defines *nationalism* as "…excessive patriotism; chauvinism … the policy or doctrine of asserting the interests of one's own nation, viewed as separate from the interests of other nations or the common interests of all nations." *Cosmopolitanism* Webster's lists as a noun derivative of *cosmopolitan,* which is "a person who is free from local, provincial, or national bias or attachment; citizen of the world; cosmopolite." Its synonyms are "sophisticated, urbane, worldly."[78] Hence, the antidote to Western nationalism is AmEuropean cosmopolitanism. Nationalism is a cultural and social habit, a root cause of the evils of war and hatred that must and can be changed. The evil of nationalism is not intrinsic to human nature; it is a learned negative cultural and social habit that is simply passed down from one generation to another.

The purpose of AmEuropean cosmopolitanism is to further peace by broadening the horizons of AmEuropeans, thereby making the peoples of North America and Europe more understanding, sophisticated, open-minded, and worldly, as they become more aware of each other's nations and cultures as well as the other nations and cultures of the world. In addition to broadening one's horizons, working and residing in foreign countries builds character by stimulating personal growth. People learn to understand the language and culture of their host country in order to acclimate themselves to their new foreign surroundings and overcome culture shock. Language is the bearer of culture and the key to the hearts of people.

A true AmEuropean cosmopolite feels at home in any AmEuropean city, which actually is not difficult to achieve, as the cultural shock is minimal for an open-minded person of the same civilization, thirsting for knowledge and savoir-faire. Most AmEuropeans grow up in the West and, therefore, have a common cultural and social history. It is fear, however, that blocks the feeling of being a cosmopolite.

AmEuropean cosmopolitanism recognizes that Western nationalism is a restrictive, divisive and destructive force. AmEuropean cosmopolitanism and AmEuropean unity are inclusive, unifying and constructive forces. AmEuropean cosmopolitanism is more adequate at developing open-mindedness, fraternity, and sophistication than its counterpart nationalism. Thus, it is a better form of thought than the separatist ideology of closed- and divisive-minded nationalism, a major cause of war. Whatever leads to war will eventually lead to the breakdown of civilization, as Toynbee points out: "War has proved to have been the proximate cause of the breakdown of every civilization."[79] Hence, to facilitate AmEuropean unity, the divisive-mindedness of Western nationalism should be overcome. The antidote to Western nationalism is AmEuropean cosmopolitanism, for to be an AmEuropean is not only of the flesh (a citizen) but also of the mind (an ideal).

In *The Story of Civilization, Volume 9, The Age of Voltaire* Will and Ariel Durant explain our great philosophers' rejection of nationalism and patriotism.

"The *philosophes* rejected nationalism and patriotism on the ground that these emotions narrowed the conceptions of humanity and moral obligation and made it easier for kings to lead their people into war. The article 'Patrie' in the Dictionnaire philosophique condemned patriotism as incorporated egotism.... Montesquieu, Voltaire, Diderot, and d'Alembert in France, like Lessing, Kant Herder, Goethe, and Schiller in Germany, were 'good Europeans,' and Frenchmen or Germans afterward. As one religion and one language had promoted cosmopolitanism in Western Europe in the Middle Ages, so cosmopolitanism developed on the Continent as a result of the spread of the French language and culture. Rousseau in 1755 spoke of 'those great cosmopolitan minds that make light of the barriers designed to sunder nation from nation, and who, like the Sovereign Power that created them, embrace all mankind within the scope of their benevolence.' Elsewhere he wrote, with characteristic exaggeration: 'There are no longer Frenchmen or Germans,… there are only Europeans.' This was true only of the nobility and the intelligentsia, but in those strata the cosmopolitan spirit extended from Paris to Naples and St. Petersburg. Even in wartime aristocrats and literati mingled with others of their class across frontiers; Hume, Horace Walpole, Gibbon, and Adam Smith were welcomed in Parisian society while England and France were at war, and the Prince de Ligne felt at home in almost any European capital. Soldiers too had a bit of this internationalism. 'Every German officer,' said Duke Ferdinand of Brunswick, 'should feel honored to serve under the French flag'; an entire regiment in the French army—the Allemands Royaux—was composed of Germans. The Revolution put an end to this cosmopolitan camaraderie of manners and minds; the ascendancy of France faded, and nationalism advanced."[80]

Extreme patriotism and nationalism engulfed Europe and the world in two world wars. Europeans have finally learned, as their eighteenth-century philosophers long ago believed, that cosmopolitanism is more adequate than nationalism and patriotism for ensuring peace. For this reason, I advise AmEuropean cosmopolitanism over Western nationalism.

In *Who Are We?* Samuel Huntington offers America three alternatives for the future: [global] cosmopolitanism, imperialism, and/or nationalism.[81] With [global] cosmopolitanism "the world reshapes America," he says; with imperialism "America remakes the world"; and with nationalism America is "devoted to the preservation and enhancement of those qualities that have defined America since its founding." The qualities defining America, he expresses in the following terms: "America is different, and that difference is defined in large part by its Anglo-Protestant culture and its religiosity." [82]

There is, however, a fourth option, a middle road hitherto unknown to Huntington. This new concept is what I call "AmEuropean cosmopolitanism." AmEuropean cosmopolitanism is the middle road between Huntington's three options for the future of United States. The three options that Huntington puts forward, however, are extremes to be guarded against. For the safety, security, and prosperity of civilization, we must take the middle road and guard against extremism. With the enormous world population coupled with the rapid means of transportation, global cosmopolitanism would slowly suffocate the diverse splendor and uniqueness of indigenous, local, regional and national societies, cultures, and eventually civilizations, thereby creating just one global culture and civilization without cultural uniqueness and diverse splendor. We must guard and protect the uniqueness and diverse splendor of civilizations, not erase them. As Huntington articulated, "America cannot become the world and still be America," and "Other peoples cannot become American and still be themselves." Imperialism with its exploitation and domination of other cultures and nations is not an option to be considered. And as for nationalism, who knows better than the Europeans as to the evils of nationalism that entangled Europe in numerous wars, culminating in the "Great War" of World War I and the "war of annihilation" and "total war" of World War II? History teaches us that nationalism leads to alienation, isolation, and protectionist tariffs that worsen economies and cause trade wars; and when the flame of nationalism is fueled further, nationalism turns into a cause of war.

Why is nationalism destructive for the survival of a civilization? Nationalism is self-centeredness, which slows progress and narrows the individual's perception and awareness of the world to his or her nation-state, as cultural, political, and economic emphasis is placed on the nation-state. Moreover, nationalism is divisive-mindedness against other nations. In this sense, it disturbs harmony like a disease and retards progress, especially in the aftermath of a war. Given the weapons of mass destruction that exist today, "nationalism is a death wish," as Toynbee indicated.[83] In *The Revolt of the Masses* Ortega y Gasset declared, "Nationalism is nothing but a mania, a pretext to escape from the necessity of inventing something new, some great enterprise. Its primitive methods of action and the type of men it exalts reveal abundantly that it is opposite of a historical creation."[84] Hence, we can passively allow nuclear mass-suicide by continuing the "mania" of nationalism, or we can actively build peace by taking the middle road of AmEuropean cosmopolitanism toward the "historical creation" of AmEuropa.

"Until our states become members of a large and effectively protective group, they will continue to act like individuals and families in the hunting stage," explained Will and Ariel Durant.[85] AmEuropa is that "large and effectively protective group" to take nation-states out of the "hunting stage" of war.

"Know thyself!" was the foremost Greek motto. To know yourself is to know your civilization. AmEuropean cosmopolitanism helps to broaden the citizen's horizons to include knowledge of the civilization in which the citizen lives and to which other AmEuropean member countries and their cultures belong. The creation of AmEuropa assists AmEuropeans in discovering the other nations that make up their civilization, thus helping AmEuropeans find themselves as a part of a whole, the civilization to which they belong. Civilization is the smallest unit that can be studied to understand history; limiting the study of history to the nation-state makes history unintelligible.[86] Knowing yourself in the context of civilization helps us to better understanding from where we came and to where we are going. Schools often place too much emphasis on the study of the nation-state and too little emphasis on the study of civilization and culture to the detriment of both civilization and the world, leaving students with cultural "blinkers" and a narrow-minded perception of the world. In *The Seekers: The Story of Man's Continuing Quest to Understand His World* Daniel Boorstin writes, "People had been taught history, H.G. Wells complained, 'in nationalist blinkers, ignoring every country but their own, and now they were turned out into a blaze'.…. In a comprehensive history of the world … he [H.G. Wells] revealed the interconnectedness and uncertainty of human destiny in the twentieth century and the need to transcend national ambitions." [87]

For the West to survive, its people must learn to "transcend national ambitions" by forging an AmEuropean identity through AmEuropean unity in the Alliance of AmEuropa. A nation-state alienated from its civilization will slowly crumble. Just as a body part cannot exist separated from the whole, a nation-state cannot exist separated from its civilization and the world.

Everyone has the right to be proud of one's homeland; consequently, nationalism and patriotism to a certain degree are healthy as long as they do not lead to arrogance, ignorance, and the hatred of other nations, which they unfortunately often do. Some philosophers like Voltaire for example would argue that arrogance and hatred of others are inherent to nationalism and patriotism and therefore are intrinsically bad. AmEuropean cosmopolitanism helps to prevent the potential arrogance and hatred of others inherent to nationalism and patriotism that may block tactful diplomacy, cooperation, partnership, bi- and multilateralism, solidarity, teamwork, unity, the aggrandizement of individual liberty and personal freedom, and peace.

Although civilizations have existed long before nation-states, some people and leaders have so idolized their nation-state that they have failed to see that the encompassing civilization of which their nation-state is part is indeed declining. Nationalism tends to blind people to the fact that if the whole (civilization) declines so too must the part (the nation-state) decline along with it.

The integration of AmEuropeans shall help familiarize member nations with other member nations, which are culturally and linguistically different from their own, thereby broadening the horizons of AmEuropeans without increasing the risk of cultural clashes and violence, as the majority of AmEuropeans were raised in a Western culture regardless of their ethnicity, race, or religion.

A study of the history and culture of other AmEuropean member countries and the ties to their former colonies offers a better understanding of the world. Even better than the study of foreign cultures, however, is to experience them. An old German adage says, *"Probieren geht über studieren":* One learns more through experience than through mere study. AmEuropean cosmopolitanism encourages the experience, and AmEuropean integration makes the experience possible.

Chapter 8
AmEuropean Citizenship

AmEuropean citizenship shall make all citizens of Alliance member countries a citizen of AmEuropa, giving all AmEuropeans a common identity regardless of ethnicity, race, or religion.

The purpose of AmEuropean citizenship is to extend the citizen's realm in which he or she may live and work. AmEuropean citizenship creates a feeling of solidarity among AmEuropeans, which accelerates the creation of an AmEuropean homeland stretching across the Atlantic for all AmEuropeans.

Just as the Alliance of AmEuropa does not replace the nation-state but complements it, AmEuropean citizenship does not replace an individual's national citizenship but complements it: that is to say, it is in addition to national citizenship. In AmEuropa, AmEuropeans can have their cake and eat it too; they can have both national citizenship and AmEuropean citizenship at the same time. AmEuropean citizenship not only gives AmEuropeans a unified, common identity but also allows AmEuropean citizens to legally live and work in any member country of AmEuropa.

The Alliance of AmEuropa is a political force of good that stretches beyond the limits of a mere nation-state. "While the state of which we happen to be citizens makes more concrete and more imperious claims on our allegiance, especially in the present age, the civilization of which we are members really counts for more in our lives. And this civilization of which we are members includes—at most stages in its history—the citizens of other states besides our own," wrote Toynbee.[88] As an entire civilization is vastly larger than a mere nation-state and existed long before the nation-state, citizenship of a civilization is vastly greater than the citizenship of a nation-state. Hence, AmEuropean citizenship is a higher form of political association than the citizenship of a nation-state, thus making the acquisition of AmEuropean citizenship yet a higher honor than the acquisition of a national citizenship.

For the citizens of Alliance member countries, the word "AmEuropa" shall be unassumingly centered at the top of the AmEuropean passport on both the cover and first page. For the citizens of the USA and Canada, the word "AmEuropa" shall be placed above the title of the nation-state, that being the United States of America or Canada. For citizens of the European Union, the word "AmEuropa" shall be placed above the words "European Union" as well as above the name of the nation-state. As a civilization is greater in size than a nation-state, AmEuropa, representing the unity of a civilization, is greater in size to the European Union or nation-state, requiring that "AmEuropa" be placed above both the words "European Union" and the name of the nation-state. The size of the font of the name of the nation-state may, however, be printed in a larger size font than the word "AmEuropa."

With the inception of an AmEuropean citizenship complementing but not replacing national and EU citizenships, AmEuropeans shall begin to have a feeling of having multiple-identities. When the word "AmEuropa" is added to the cover of AmEuropean national passports, Americans and Canadians shall adopt a secondary AmEuropean identity, and EU citizens shall adapt a tertiary AmEuropean identity, thus reflecting the unity of the West. The adoption of an AmEuropean identity shall make the nations of the Alliance feel closer to their fellow partner-nations and compatriots in AmEuropa and Western civilization. AmEuropeans shall recognize that they are part of a larger family on both sides of the Atlantic. As AmEuropeans move more and more both ways across the Atlantic, the feeling of having two or three identities shall help to increase solidarity among member nations. People will be able to more easily identify with and relate to a greater number of peoples, cultures, and nations. This is a positive change, as a feeling of having multiple-identities increases harmony among cultures and nations.

AmEuropean citizenship shall help to broaden the horizons of AmEuropeans, as it will facilitate travel by allowing the AmEuropean citizen to stay in another member country as a resident for an unlimited period of time instead of the short three-month limit without a legal work permit currently allowed by most countries in North America and Europe.

With the inception of AmEuropean citizenship Americans, Canadians, Britons, and Europeans shall no longer only be Americans, Canadians, Britons, and Europeans but also "AmEuropeans."

Chapter 9
AmEuropeanism, AmEuropeanist, the AmEuropean Movement

AmEuropeanism is the belief in AmEuropean unity through the creation of the Alliance of AmEuropa, the AmEuropean Greater Common Market, and the AmEuropean Area of Freedom.

AmEuropeanism is dedicated to the goal of improving relations between North America and Europe as well as among Atlantic alliance (NATO) member countries. Through AmEuropean unity and AmEuropean integration, AmEuropeanism seeks to improve cooperation and partnership among nations, secure peace, and enhance individual liberty, personal freedom, equality, open-mindedness, tolerance, and human rights. In addition, AmEuropeanism seeks to broaden the horizons of AmEuropeans by encouraging AmEuropean cosmopolitism through the free movement of citizens in AmEuropa.

AmEuropeanism includes a belief in the voluntary unity and integration of AmEuropeans—all citizens of AmEuropa regardless of race, creed, color, sexual orientation, or class—and in affording AmEuropeans the right to live and work legally in any member country of AmEuropa. Achieving the AmEuropean Area of Freedom—the area in which the free movement of goods, services, capital, and citizens is permitted and encouraged among member countries of AmEuropa while keeping border controls where desired—is a preeminent goal of AmEuropeanism.

AmEuropeanism incorporates the ideal of creating solidarity within the West by alleviating the destructive divisive-mindedness of nationalism among Western nation-states through the creation of the Alliance of AmEuropa.

To ensure the survival of all civilizations, AmEuropeanism strives to revive Western civilization as well as to preserve the existence of other civilizations. AmEuropeanism strives to guard and protect the uniqueness and splendor of all civilizations and their cultures, not to eliminate them by creating one global civilization. AmEuropeanism recognizes the existence of a common cultural identity in Western civilization and the need to create harmony and solidarity among Atlantic alliance nations for the survival of the West and world peace. To this end, AmEuropeanism strives to strengthen the West and revitalize its cultural and scientific creativity and inquiry by facilitating the exchange of ideas through AmEuropean unity, AmEuropean cosmopolitanism, and AmEuropean integration.

The enemies of the West, the threat of terrorism, and the rise in strength of authoritarian communist China afford North America and Europe the opportunity to unite for two major common causes: survival and peace. Peace as well as the survival of civilizations, the West and the Atlantic alliance take precedence over personal political disputes between heads of governments. The survival of life and civilizations are at stake, not only one or two nation-states.

AmEuropeanism is the philosophical and political principle of building a common AmEuropa, an AmEuropean homeland for all AmEuropeans regardless of race, creed, or color. This AmEuropean homeland is to be made up of nation-states, exemplifying cooperation and partnership, in which individual liberty and personal freedom is enhanced to an unparalleled degree in the history of mankind.

Inherent to AmEuropeanism and AmEuropean cosmopolitanism is the freedom from national constraints and arrogance, including the arrogance of nationalism, a major cause of war. The liberty and freedom from national constraints will release a renaissance of creativity and aesthetics in all the creative arts as well as in science and technology. AmEuropeanism increases cooperation among peoples and most importantly endows AmEuropeans with the right to free movement within a vast area of freedom that stretches from the western coast of the United States and Canada to the eastern boarders of Finland, Poland, and Hungary.

AmEuropeanism shall encompass the AmEuropean Movement in literature, politics, philosophy, and the arts as a means of promoting AmEuropean unity, AmEuropean cosmopolitanism, AmEuropean integration, and the Alliance of AmEuropa.

The cosmopolitan ideals of philosophers, literati, and other thinkers of earlier more cosmopolitan centuries prior to the rise of nationalism has influenced my concept of AmEuropeanism with its AmEuropean cosmopolitanism. Moreover, unlike Communism, which sacrifices liberty for equality and justice, AmEuropeanism rewards greater liberty for greater equality and justice.

The purpose of AmEuropeanism is to develop a set of peaceful political and philosophical principles and guidelines contributing to AmEuropean unity, AmEuropean cosmopolitanism, and the creation of the Alliance of AmEuropa for greater peace, prosperity, and freedom. Central to AmEuropeanism is a belief in the free movement of goods, services, capital, and citizens among member countries of the Alliance of AmEuropa contributing to the goal of long-term peace, as the integration of peoples and economies leads to the cooperation and partnership of governments. Through the creation of the Alliance of AmEuropa, AmEuropeanism seeks to exemplify cooperation, cultural diversity, inclusiveness, individual liberty, open-mindedness, partnership, personal freedom, prosperity, security, social justice, tolerance, teamwork, and peace.

An AmEuropeanist

An AmEuropeanist is an Atlanticist who believes in the principles of AmEuropeanism, which include AmEuropean unity, AmEuropean cosmopolitanism, and AmEuropean integration through the creation of the Alliance of AmEuropa.

The AmEuropean Movement

With this manifesto commences the AmEuropean Movement. The AmEuropean Movement seeks to improve relations between North America and Europe and especially among the Atlantic alliance (NATO) member countries, for the Atlantic alliance is vital for the survival of civilization, the West, and securing peace. The AmEuropean Movement is a peaceful, nonpartisan, democratic movement for AmEuropean unity, the unity of North America and Europe, including NATO member counties, to be achieved progressively through the creation of the Alliance of AmEuropa, an alliance of the United States of America, Canada, and the European Union. AmEuropean integration, including the free movement of goods, services, capital, and citizens (those holding citizenship of an Alliance member county) among member countries of AmEuropa, is central to the AmEuropean Movement.

Chapter 10
Alliance Member Countries and Proposed Accession Requirements

The envisioned founding member countries of AmEuropa are the United States of America and Canada in North America and twenty-five of the twenty-seven EU member states of Austria, Belgium, Cyprus, Czech Republic, Denmark, Estonia, Finland, France, Germany, Greece, Hungary, Ireland, Italy, Latvia, Lithuania, Luxembourg, Malta, Poland, Portugal, the Netherlands, Slovakia, Slovenia, Spain, Sweden, and the United Kingdom in Europe. Other European and North American nations may be admitted into the Alliance if they so democratically and voluntarily desire, meet all the requirements for accession, and are accepted unanimously by all other member countries.

Presently, twenty-one of the twenty-six NATO countries should be founding member countries of the Alliance of AmEuropa with the exception of Bulgaria, Romania, Iceland, Norway, and Turkey, as they are either not an EU member state or do not have a free movement of people or citizens agreement with all EU member states. As mentioned in chapter one, Bulgaria and Romania entered the EU on January 1, 2007, but not all EU member states will grant Bulgarians and Romanians the right to live and work freely in all EU member states for some time to come. For this reason, Bulgaria and Romania would not yet meet the preliminary requirements for accession into the Alliance. In addition, Turkey would not yet meet the preliminary requirements for accession into the Alliance, as it is not yet an EU member state, a signatory of the Schengen Agreement (permitting the free movement of people without border controls among Schengen member states), and does not have an independent bilateral free movement of people or citizens agreement with the EU. Iceland and Norway, both NATO members, signatories of the Schengen Agreement, and having strong and stable economies, could theoretically become members of the Alliance of AmEuropa, but, as they are not EU member states, it is unlikely they would wish to be founding member countries of AmEuropa. As the U.S. Congress approved the building of a seven hundred-mile wall between Mexico and the U.S. in 2006, it is highly unlikely that Congress would seek a freedom of movement agreement with Mexico for some time to come. For Bulgaria, Romania, Mexico, and Turkey to become member countries of AmEuropa, they should first be required to have a free movement of people or citizens agreement (such as the Schengen Agreement for example) with all member states of the EU or with the United States and Canada. In addition, these countries should have to meet all the economic, social security and welfare requirements for accession as well as be accepted by all other member countries of the Alliance. Becoming a NATO member would greatly improve Mexico's chances of being accepted into the Alliance by the other member countries. The goal of joining the Alliance would give the governments of Bulgaria, Romania, Mexico, and Turkey an incentive to improve the quality of life of their people and to reduce any governmental corruption that may exist. As AmEuropa is an alliance supporting the solidarity of the nations of the Atlantic alliance (NATO) as well as the nations of North America and Europe, other North American and European countries—such as Switzerland and Norway for example—should be allowed to join the Alliance if they wish, meet all the accession requirements, and are accepted by all other member countries.

Admission into AmEuropa is to be achieved democratically. Each nation-state must vote upon accession. Once a country meets all the requirements for admission into the Alliance of AmEuropa, a vote can be cast in either a nation's Congress or Parliament or in a referendum by the people, however the country's leader's and representatives choose to decide.

Parliaments and Congress shall ultimately determine the specific admission and accession requirements for entry into the Alliance. All member countries should then be required to ratify the requirements. To ensure the success of the Alliance, a candidate country should meet the following suggested requirements:

1. A candidate country must be willing to accept the free movement of goods, services, capital, and citizens with all other member countries of the Alliance, as this is the basic principle of the Alliance. This freedom of movement principle would include the abolition of trade tariffs and quotas among member countries while retaining border controls wherever desired.

2. A candidate country should be a free democracy ranking in the top tier of freedom, providing the highest level of freedom and human rights and the least amount of corruption. One should not mix repressive governments or corrupt governments with free democracies in an alliance of free movement of goods, capital, services, and citizens. To do so would gravely endanger the governments and peoples of free democracies. Repressive and corrupt governments will often do whatever it takes to remain in power, even if it means committing mass murder. If repressive governments are willing to kill their own compatriots to stay in power, then they would be willing to harm the peoples of free democracies if given the chance, for they perceive democratic governments as a threat to the existence of their own repressive and corrupt regimes. Hence, an alliance of free movement should require that candidate member countries be in the highest "freedom" ranking in freedom indexes such as *Freedom in the World* published by Freedom House.[89]

3. In Europe, a candidate country should be willing to enter the European Union or become a signatory of the Schengen Agreement or have some other form of bilateral agreement with the EU, permitting the free movement of people or citizens with all EU member states, before becoming an Alliance member country. In North America, a candidate country should be willing to have a free movement of people or citizens agreement with the United States and Canada before becoming an Alliance member country.

In all cases, all candidate countries should be accepted by all member countries before entry into the Alliance is effectuated.

4. A candidate country should be an Atlantic alliance (NATO) member but it is not mandatory if it is a member state of the EU, a signatory of the Schengen Agreement, or has some other free movement of people or citizens agreement with all EU member states or Canada and the U.S.

5. A candidate country should have a social security and welfare system comparable to those in Europe, Canada, or the United States. There would be no incentive for a nation to join an alliance if it knew that other member nations could take advantage of its social security and welfare system. For this reason, all member countries should have an adequate and comparable social security and welfare system.

6. A candidate country should have a free market economy.

7. A candidate country should have a standard of living comparable to other AmEuropean countries. (Exact figures should be determined by Parliaments and Congress.)

8. A candidate country should have achieved a high level of economic development, including a stable economy and a stable currency. (Exact figures should be determined by Parliaments and Congress.)

9. A candidate country should have low crime, corruption and inflation rates as well as a low budget deficit as a percentage of its GDP. (Exact

figures should be determined by Parliaments and Congress.)

10. A candidate country should adhere to the "principles of liberty, democracy, respect for human rights and fundamental freedoms, [including the protection of minorities], and the rule of law."[90]

11. In foresight, to prevent any cultural clashes that could possibly arise due to the free movement of citizens, only countries with governments embracing Western values, such as democracy, equality, liberty, and freedom—including freedom of speech, freedom of press, and freedom of religion—should be considered for entry into the Alliance.

The aforementioned requirements should be followed to ensure the success of the Alliance, its common market and its area of freedom. In addition, before a new country can be accepted into the Alliance, all other member countries must consent to it through a vote by Congress or Parliament or a referendum by the people. A vote conducted by the elected officials of the nation's government or by the people themselves in the form of a national referendum is for each nation to decide. There would be no incentive for a country to join an alliance in which it has no say; consequently, each nation, regardless of size, must have a say as to which countries are allowed to join the Alliance. In this way, no nation would feel forced to accept that which it does not agree to. Nonetheless, the possibility of membership should be open to all countries of North America and Europe if they meet all the accession requirements. AmEuropa stands for unity and inclusiveness.

As NAFTA does not allow for the free movement of citizens or people, AmEuropa cannot be likened to NAFTA. In addition, AmEuropa differs from the European Union in many vital aspects. The following are examples of how they differ:

1. AmEuropa is an alliance, the EU a union. Webster's New Universal Unabridged Dictionary defines "alliance" as "a formal agreement or treaty between two or more nations to cooperate for specific purposes; a merging of efforts or interests by persons, families, states, or organizations." A "union" it defines as "a group of states or nations united into one political body. Union implies an alliance so close and permanent that the separate states or parties become essentially one."

2. AmEuropa is not to have a central, federal government; in many ways the EU does in Brussels.

3. AmEuropa is not to have a supranational currency union; the EU does with the euro.

4. Although both AmEuropa and the EU benefit the world through increased commerce, cooperation, foreign aid, security, stability, and peace, AmEuropa benefits first and foremost AmEuropeans and the EU, Europeans.

Working together in AmEuropa, America, Canada, and the European Union shall be forces of good, supporting democracy, equality, and human rights throughout the world. It is, however, human nature to criticize that which is new by saying "It won't work." Prominent people are fallible and sometimes wrong, as was Dr. Henry Kissinger regarding the euro. "In 1999, Henry

Kissinger opined that the euro was one of those good ideas that would not come to fruition, because the people of Europe would never accept it."[91] Since shortly after its tangible inception on January 1, 2002, the euro has gone from being worth $0.88 U.S. cents on Jan. 18, 2002 to $1.34 U.S. dollars on January 10, 2007.[92] In the same way, those who criticize the Alliance of AmEuropa by saying "It won't work" shall be wrong, as was Dr. Henry Kissinger about the euro. Hence, to guarantee the success of the Alliance in the face of pessimists, each candidate member country should be required to meet all the accession requirements so as not to become a burden upon the economies, social security and welfare systems, and peoples of the other member countries. After all, it is the people who pay the taxes for their governments to survive. For this reason, we cannot expect or demand to burden the citizens of any partner nation with the problems and expenses of another nation's undemocratic government or unstable, weak economy. As the standard of living of the U.S., Canada, and the EU are similar, none can accuse the others of trying to take advantage of its economy and social system; that is to say, the U.S., Canada, or the EU cannot accuse any of the other two of being an economic burden. Hence, it is vital that the founding countries of AmEuropa have strong economies, stable currencies, and developed social security and welfare systems as well as be free and stable democracies.

Conclusion

The sum total of influence and power the West can exercise and muster is equivalent to the amount of unity and harmony with which North America and Europe are committed and coordinated. The Alliance of AmEuropa shall seek to commit and coordinate the two continents to good ends only, such as development assistance, humanitarian aid, prosperity development (i.e. wealth creation), defending human rights, and peacekeeping.

The greatness of AmEuropa is, therefore, to be achieved not through war, but through peace, not by conquest, but by alliance. In the Age of Amity, the "light of reason" shall reign supreme over the darkness of ignorance and fear. Equally, the humbleness and cooperation of alliance shall supersede the arrogance and self-centeredness of nationalism, a major cause of war.

Just as both the divisive nationalistic ideals and pessimistic thought of the twentieth century led to the death of an old Europe and the renewed cosmopolitan ideals of previous centuries resulted in the rebirth a new Europe, the ideals of fraternity, equality, liberty, and freedom coupled with the success of Europe's free movement agreements, shall lead the West to AmEuropean unity and the creation of AmEuropa. If European countries, just five years after the hostility and destruction of World

War II, could put aside their animosities and commence European unity with the Schuman Declaration launching the European Coal and Steel Community (ECSC), then the building of AmEuropa shall not be a problem, as such animosity among Western nations no longer exists. The devastation of World War II caused a "transformation of the European mind and spirit" that would bury the egotistical ambitions of nationalism and patriotism inherent to power politics and result in European unity.[93] This transformation of mind and spirit would take two centuries. Europeans would finally call themselves not only Frenchmen and Germans but also Europeans, as did the cosmopolitan *philosophes,* literati, thinkers, and other intellectuals had done up to the early nineteenth century.

To flourish as a civilization, the West must creatively and harmoniously self determine its own future. We must stop emphasizing our differences and start emphasizing our similarities. By affirming our similarities as a civilization through the creation of AmEuropa, AmEuropean unity gives the West the power to self determine its own destiny.

The freedom for the average North American and European to live and work on both continents is a freedom that is still missing in Western society today; yet it once existed during much of the seventeenth, eighteenth, and even nineteenth centuries. Hence, this would not be a new freedom but a reinstatement of a former freedom that had been taken away.

Excuses for not wanting to build the Alliance of AmEuropa have their roots in arrogance, closed-mindedness, complacency, fear, hate, laziness, or self-centeredness. These are the true obstacles to building AmEuropa.

If we can learn to reject these negative emotions and character traits, then we will be able to easily overcome any obstacles that may arise.

Respect for human dignity and a regard for the well-being of others should include the desire to peacefully enhance the individual liberty and personal freedom of others. Open-mindedness and a positive attitude are important for progress and thus important to comprehend the benefits that AmEuropean unity would afford individuals and companies as well as the West and the world.

Joint venture is the way of the future. Only working together in AmEuropa can the West truly advance civilization, stimulate creativity and intellectual inquiry, defend human rights, and keep parity with China. Unlike the European Union, which grew out of war to preclude war, AmEuropa is to be the result of peace and not of war; thus, it would behoove the West to overcome apathy and discord without the necessity of war to push forward unity. For the survival of civilizations, the growth of freedom and prosperity, the assurance of stability and security, and the advancement of peace as well as to effectively coordinate development assistance and humanitarian aid in the world, the political and economic solidarity of the West must become a reality. This can only be achieved through AmEuropean unity and AmEuropean integration. To this end, the people of AmEuropa shall no longer be only Americans, Canadians, Britons or Europeans but also "AmEuropeans." AmEuropeans, having a common past in Western civilization and a common cause in peace and liberty, shall too have a common future in AmEuropa.

In AmEuropa, a citizen's homeland grows from the size of one nation-state (or the European Union for some Europeans) to the size of almost an entire civilization, including twenty-seven nation-states stretching across two continents, without ever having inflicted misery, the loss of territory, or the lost of wealth upon another nation. Therein shall lie the greatness of AmEuropa. AmEuropa is an alliance that shall be founded in peace, through peace, for peace and the extension of individual liberty and personal freedom. The creation of an AmEuropean homeland brought forth by the Alliance of AmEuropa for all AmEuropeans is our future.

The Alliance of AmEuropa is the worldly savior of the West. America, Canada, and the European Union, together as the Alliance of AmEuropa, form a trilogy of strength. Facilitating commerce and the exchange of ideas through the integration of its citizens, the West can flourish on a grand scale as never before.

We must not resist change, for change is a law of life and nature. To resist change is to resist progress and nature itself. Resistance to change is based on fear, the fear of the future and the unknown. Everything new, even love, frightens at first.[94] Hence, if you may find this concept of AmEuropa fear provoking at first, it is merely because it is new. A positive attitude and a little open-mindedness and understanding will remedy that. "...After all," wrote Kagan, "it is more than a cliché that the United States and Europe share a set of common Western beliefs. Their aspirations for humanity are much the same, even if their vast disparity of power has now put them in very different places. Perhaps it is not too naively optimistic to believe that a little common understanding could still go a long way."[95] "Mankind's past successes," wrote Toynbee, "in bringing once sovereign independent States into voluntary union with one another are guarantees that we possess the experience and technique for achieving the great work of political construction that is now demanded of us. We have the ability if we have the will. Our fate lies in our own hands."[96]

AmEuropa and NATO, together, shall form the core and bulwark of the West. Hence, AmEuropa, as the deepening of the Atlantic alliance (NATO), shall defend the values that the West stands for—such as democracy, equality, liberty, and freedom—not only as separate nation-states but also as a cohesive civilization. If civilizations should nevermore be allowed to decline and fall, then it is our responsibility to ensure the survival of Western civilization. If we do not, no one else will. May AmEuropean unity bring the people of North America and Europe together before it is "too late!"

North America and Europe are the two pillars of Western civilization; thus, if divided, the West cannot stand. Equally, an incessant failure to unite would constitute the demise of the West in the face of the enemies of the West and the rising Chinese Communist Party in world affairs. Unity is strength! Only through AmEuropa can the U.S. and EU remain superpowers and prevent China's authoritarian, repressive communistic government from becoming the next world leader. Moreover, only through AmEuropean unity can the West effectively champion human rights. The future of the West and the world lies in our hands. Let it not be forgotten: United we stand, divided we fall! Discord leads to division, decay, and death. Unity is growth, love, and life.

The West must lead by setting a good example of harmony, teamwork, and unity. In AmEuropa, no nation shall ever be alone. A commitment to AmEuropa is a commitment to securing peace; saving civilizations, including the West; and extending individual liberty and personal freedom.

If the Europeans with their long history of wars could more or less unite under one European government in Brussels, then forming a loose alliance of Western nations, all having a similar and intertwined history, should be no problem if the force of love is stronger than the force of hate. AmEuropa is the will of love. We must learn to respect the mosaic of cultures and civilizations that make this world interesting and beautiful. Hence, like any other culture and civilization, we must not let the good things in Western civilization that our ancestors laboriously created, built, and died for decline and fall and be done in vain.

It takes time to build unity. Rome was not built in a day. With resolve, diligence, determination, perseverance, tact, and respect, we can achieve AmEuropean unity in our lifetime. Where there is a will, there is a way! AmEuropa, as a political force of unity, is a powerful force of love and strength.

For the love of peace and civilization as well as for the victory of individual liberty and personal freedom, North Americans and Europeans, unite! After all, in AmEuropa we shall all be AmEuropeans: one people, one flag, one alliance!

When the peoples of North America and Europe are reunited in AmEuropa, AmEuropeans and the West shall be one and indivisible. In AmEuropa, America, Canada, and the European Union shall be like Alexander Dumas' three musketeers "all for one and one for all!" Let the AmEuropean Movement begin! and AmEuropa shall be the achievement of open-mindedness, the accomplishment of teamwork, the advancement of equality, and the fulfillment of freedom. In sum, AmEuropa shall be a victory of peace and the triumph of love!

 *The AmEuropa Doctrine*

The AmEuropa Doctrine is dedicated to the goal of unity within the Alliance of AmEuropa. AmEuropa, a contraction of the continents of North America and Europe, endeavors to develop solidarity among its nations and citizens and the world to preclude war and the decline of civilizations. Hence, the supporters of the Alliance of AmEuropa are committed to the following:

1. The establishment of AmEuropa: the alliance of Canada, the European Union, and the United States of America called the Alliance of AmEuropa.
2. The free movement of goods, services, capital, and citizens (while retaining border controls where desired) between all member countries of the Alliance, as the integration of nations and economies leads to the cooperation of governments.

3. The creation of an AmEuropean citizenship to complement an individual's national citizenship, thereby permitting a citizen of AmEuropa—henceforth called an "AmEuropean"—to live and work in any member country of AmEuropa.
4. The emergence of a cosmopolitan AmEuropean citizen, achieved by the cooperation, integration, and unity of AmEuropeans in the Alliance.
5. The freedom, inclusiveness, and unity of AmEuropeans in an alliance achieved peacefully and democratically, thereby paving the way for world peace.[97]

Notes

[1] Jean Monnet's quotation translated by Kent M. Chater.

Introduction
[2] **Chater,** *AmEuropa: Love and Betrayal in the Greatest Alliance of Nations,* **1-8.**
[3] **Angel, Lafitte,** *L'Europe,* **11.**
[4] **Ibid., 100.**
[5] **Schnabel, Rocca,** *The Next Superpower,* **91.**
[6] **Huntington,** *The Clash of Civilizations and the Remaking of World Order,* **46-47.**
[7] **Chomsky,** *Hegemony or Survival,* **12.**
[8] **Reid,** *The United States of Europe,* **6.**
[9] **Kagan,** *Of Paradise and Power,* **101-102.**
[10] **Fukuyama,** *America at the Crossroads,* **189.**
[11] **Huntington,** *The Clash of Civilizations and the Remaking of World Order,* **307.**
[12] **Schnabel, Rocca,** *The Next Superpower,* **75.**
[13] **Chater,** *AmEuropa: Love and Betrayal in the Greatest Alliance of Nations,* **3.**
[14] **Although differing greatly, the European Union's single market and its Area of Freedom, Security and Justice (AFSJ) inspired my concepts of the AmEuropean Greater Common Market and AmEuropean Area of Freedom. For more information, see: Pinder,** *The European Union,* **60, 102, 182; or European Union, "Delegation of the European Commission to the United States," website:** http://www.eurunion.org/

Chapter 1: What is AmEuropa?
[15] **Pinder,** *The European Union,* **182.**
[16] **Toynbee,** *Change and Habit: The Challenge of Our Time,* **34-35.**

[17] **Fukuyama,** *America at the Crossroads: Democracy, Power, and the Neoconservative Legacy,* **157,159.**

[18] **TransAtlantic Business Dialogue (TABD),** *"About the TABD,"* **website:** http://www.tabd.com/about.

[19] **Phrase inspired by Jean Monnet's « Nous ne coalisons pas des Etats; ne unissons de hommes. »**

[20] **Although differing slightly, the European Union's four freedoms inspired my concept of the AmEuropean four freedoms. For more information, see: Pinder,** *The European Union,* **102, 188; or European Union, "Delegation of the European Commission to the United States," website:** http://www.eurunion.org/.

[21] **July 2006 estimate. CIA,** *The World Factbook 2007,* **website:** https://www.cia.gov/cia/publications/factbook/index.html, **February 8, 2007.**

[22] **2006 estimates. CIA,** *The World Factbook 2007,* **website:** https://www.cia.gov/cia/publications/factbook/index.html, **updated February 8, 2007. The CIA's export figures are calculated on a free on board (f.o.b.) basis that is based on the official exchange rate rather than the purchasing power parity. For an explanation of terms, see same website.**

[23]**"Democracy, freedom, liberty, peace, security, and the rule of law" are values set forth in the North Atlantic Treaty of 1949.**

[24] **NATO.** *The North Atlantic Treaty,* **Article 5.**

[25] **Huntington,** *The Clash of Civilizations and the Remaking of World Order,* **194-195.**

[26] **InfoPlease: All the Knowledge You Need,** *The World's Most Repressive Societies,* **website:** http://www.infoplease.com/ipa/A0933891.html.

[27] **Immigration Service Center, "Immigrant Visas," website:** http://www.infodomain.com/immigran2.htm.

[28] **Embassy of the United States, Budapest, Hungary; website:** http://budapest.usembassy.gov/immigrant_application.html.

[29] **Durant, Durant,** *The Lessons of History,* **audiocassette.**

[30] **Gedmin, "Europe and NATO: Saving the Alliance" in** *Present Dangers,* **196.**

[31] **Organization of African Unity,** *Treaty Establishing the African Economic Community,* **1-3, 11, 65.**

Chapter 2: Will Unity Come Too Late?

[32] **Ortega y Gasset,** *Revolt of the Masses,* **150.**

[33] **Toynbee,** *Civilization on Trial,* **58, 60-62.**

[34] **Toynbee,** *Change and Habit: The Challenge of Our Time,* **98.**

[35] **Durant, Durant,** *The Lessons of History,* **audiocassette.**

[36] **Schnabel, Rocca,** *The Next Superpower,* **39.**

Chapter 3: AmEuropean Unity

[37] **Lloyd,** *The Passport,* **6.**

[38] **Ibid., 56.**

[39] **Spengler's notion is that civilizations grow and die as do organisms. Spengler,** *The Decline of the West.*

[40] **Ortega y Gasset,** *Revolt of the Masses,* **182-184.**

[41] **U.S. Census 2000, website:** www.census.gov/prod/ 2004pubs/c2kbr-35.pdf.

[42] **Ortega y Gasset,** *Revolt of the Masses,* **27.**

[43] **Toynbee,** *Change and Habit: The Challenge of Our Time,* **87, 90.**

[44] **NATO,** *The North Atlantic Treaty,* **website:** http://www.nato.int/ docu/basictxt/treaty.htm.

Chapter 4: AmEuropa, the Next Superpower—Keeping Ahead of China

[45] **Reid,** *The United State of Europe,* **4.**

[46] **Schnabel, Rocca,** *The Next Superpower,* **28.**

[47] **2006 estimates. CIA,** *The World Factbook 2007,* **website:** https:// www.cia.gov/cia/publications/factbook/index.html, **updated February 8, 2007. See explanation of terms on same website for definitions of GDP (PPP) and GDP (OER).**

[48] **Reid,** *The United States of Europe,* **244, 189-190. Rifkin, The European Union, 304. Schnabel, Rocca,** *The Next Superpower,* **57-58.**

[49] **Reid,** *The Untied States of Europe.* **195-196.**

[50] **Munro, "China: The Challenge of a Rising Power" in** *Present Dangers,* **47-48.**

[51] **Fukuyama,** *America at the Crossroads,* **174.**

[52] **Huntington,** *The Clash of Civilizations and the Remaking of World Order,* **312-313.**

[53] **Fukuyama,** *America at the Crossroads,* **41-42.**

[54] **Huntington,** *Clash of Civilizations and the Remaking of World Order,* **196-197.**

[55] **InfoPlease: All the Knowledge You Need,** *Freedom in the World 2005,* **website:** http://www.infoplease.com/ipa/A0930918.html.

[56] **Birkle, Gretchen, Acting Principal Deputy Assistant Secretary for Democracy, Human Rights, and Labor.**
Testimony Before the House Committee on International Relations, Subcommittee on Africa, Global Human Rights and International Operations, Washington, D.C., July 21, 2005. Website: http://www.state.gov/g/drl/rls/rm/2005/50110.htm.

Chapter 5: How to Prevent the Downfall of the West and the End of Western Culture

[57] **Spengler,** *Decline of the West,* **title; Buchanan,** *Death of the West,* **title; Barzun,** *From Dawn to Decadence,* **ix; Kagan,** *Of Paradise and Power,* **97.**

[58] **Barzun,** *From Dawn to Decadence,* **ix.**

[59] **Ibid., xvi.**

[60] **Huntington,** *The Clash of Civilizations and the Remaking of World Order,* **307.**

[61] **Toynbee,** *Change and Habit: The Challenge of Our Time,* **151.**

[62] **Ibid., 19.**

[63] **Huntington,** *The Clash of Civilizations and the Remaking of World Order,* **320-321.**

[64] **Kant,** *Perpetual Peace: A Philosophical Sketch,* **website:** http://www.mtholyoke.edu/acad/intrel/kant/kant1.htm. **Rifkin,** *The European Dream,* **298.**

[65] **Reid,** *The United States of Europe,* **22. Chomsky,** *Hegemony or Survival,* **back matter (p.305). "Hyperpower" is a term coined by Hubert Védrine in 1998; Heisbourg,** *La fin de l'Occident?,* **18.**

[66] **Heisbourg,** *La fin de l'Occident?,* **title.**

[67] **CIA.** *The World Factbook 2007,* **website:** https://www.cia.gov/cia/publications/factbook/geos/ee.html#Econ, **updated February 8, 2007.**

[68] **The White House: Office of the Press Secretary, June 26, 2004. "Fact Sheet: U.S.-EU Summit: Strengthening the Transatlantic Economic Partnership." Website:** http://www.whitehouse.gov/news/releases/2004/06/20040626-7.html.

[69] **Reid,** *The United States of Europe,* **115.**

[70] **RTR,** *Der Tagesspiegel,* **26 Januar 2007,** *Wirtschaft* **(Business section), Seite (page) 19.**

Chapter 6: The AmEuropean Greater Common Market and the AmEuropean Area of Freedom
[71] **TransAtlantic Business Dialogue,** *U.S.–EU Economic Ministerial: TABD Submission to Governments, December 7, 2006:* **"TABD November 2006, U.S.–EU Economic Ministerial Meeting," 4. Website:** http://www.tabd.com/.
[72] Bartlett, "The President's Rotten Record on Trade," website: http://www.reason.com/news/show/36683.html
[73] **Wikipedia, "Nationalism," website:** http://en.wikipedia.org/wiki/Nationalism.
[74] **Reid,** *The United States of Europe,* **123.**
[75] **TransAtlantic Business Dialogue, "Towards a Barrier-Free Transatlantic Market: Report and Recommendations to the 2006 EU-US Summit Leaders," i. Website:** http://www.tabd.com/.

Chapter 7: AmEuropean Cosmopolitanism
[76] **Toynbee,** *Change and Habit: The Challenge of Our Time,* **111, 112, 199.**
[77] **Nietzsche,** *Beyond Good and Evil: Prelude to a Philosophy of the Future,* **386.**
[78] **Webster's New Universal Unabridged Dictionary, 1279, 457.**
[79] **Toynbee,** *War and Civilization,* **vii.**
[80] **Durant, Durant,** *The Story of Civilization, Volume 9, The Age of Voltaire,* **779-780.**
[81] **Huntington,** *Who Are We?* **362.**
[82] **Ibid., 363, 365.**
[83] **Toynbee,** *Change and Habit: The Challenge of Our Time,* **112.**
[84] **Ortega y Gasset,** *The Revolt of the Masses,* **183.**
[85] **Durant, Durant,** *The Lessons of History,* **audiocassette.**
[86] **Toynbee,** *Civilization on Trial,* **195.**
[87] **Boorstin,** *The Seekers: The Story of Man's Continuing Quest to Understand His World.,* **201.**

Chapter 8: AmEuropean Citizenship
[88] Toynbee, *Civilization on Trial,* 196.

Chapter 9: AmEuropeanism, an AmEuropeanist, the AmEuropean Movement

Chapter 10: Alliance Member Countries and Proposed Accession Requirements
[89] Freedom House, *Freedom in the World 2005.* Website: InfoPlease, All the Knowledge You Need, http://www.infoplease.com/ipa/A0930918.html.
[90] Pinder, *The European Union,* 124.
[91] Reid, *The United States of Europe,* 4-5.
[92] German Embassy Washington, D.C., *The Euro,* website: http://www.germany.info/relaunch/info/publications/infocus/euro/essentials.html.

Conclusion
[93] Kagan, *Of Paradise and Power,* 53-56.
[94] Idea inspired by *"Jedes Neue, auch das Glück, erschreckt":* *"Everything new, even happiness, strikes terror."* Schiller, Johann Christoph Friedrich von. *Die Braut von Messina,* zweiter Aufzug, zweiter Auftritt.
[95] Kagan, *Of Paradise and Power,* 103.
[96] Toynbee, *War and Civilization,* xii.

"The AmEuropa Doctrine"
[97] Chater, *AmEuropa: Love and Betrayal in the Greatest Alliance of Nations,* 1.

Bibliography

Angel, Benjamin, and Jacques Lafitte. *L'Europe: Petite histoire d'une grande idée.* Paris: Découvertes Gallimard, 1999.

Bartlett, Bruce. "The President's Rotten Record on Trade, June 2006." Website: http://www.reason.com/news/show/36683.html, 2007.

Barzun, Jacques. *The Culture We Deserve.* Middletown: Wesleyan University Press, 1989.

———. *From Dawn to Decadence: 500 Years of Western Cultural Life.* New York: HarperCollins, 2000.

———. *Of Human Freedom.* New York: J.B. Lippincott Company, 1964.

Barzun, Jacques, and Michael Murray, ed. *A Jacques Barzun Reader.* New York: HarperCollins, 2002.

Birkle, Gretchen (Acting Principal Deputy Assistant Secretary for Democracy, Human Rights, and Labor). "Testimony before the House Committee on International Relations," Subcommittee on Africa, Global Human Rights and International Operations. Washington, D.C., July 21, 2005. Website: http://www.state.gov/g/drl/rls/rm/2005/50110.htm, 2007.

Boorstin, Daniel J. *The Seekers: The Story of Man's Continuing Quest to Understand His World.* New York: Random House, 1989.

Brunn, Gerhard. *Die Europäische Einigung.* Stuttgart: Reclam, 2002.

Buchanan, Patrick J. *The Death of the West*. New York: St. Martin's Press, 2002.

Chater, Kent M. *AmEuropa: Love and Betrayal in the Greatest Alliance of Nations*. Bloomington, IN: AuthorHouse, 2006.

Chomsky, Noam. *Hegemony or Survival: America's Quest for Global Dominance*. London: Penguin Books, 2004.

CIA (Central Intelligence Agency). *The World Factbook 2007*. Website: https://www.cia.gov/cia/publications/factbook/, updated February 8, 2007.

Durant, Will. *Heroes of History*. New York: Simon & Schuster, 2001.

———. *The Story of Philosophy*. New York: Pocket Books, 1991.

Durant, Will, and John Little, ed. *The Greatest Minds and Ideas of All Time*. New York: Simon & Schuster, 2002.

Durant, Will, and Ariel Durant. *Interpretations of Life*. New York: Simon & Schuster, 1970.

———. *The Lessons of History*. Auburn: The Audio Partners Publishing Corp., 1994.

———. *The Story of Civilization, Part 6: The Reformation*. New York: Simon and Schuster, 1957.

———. *The Story of Civilization, Part 7: The Age of Reason Begins*. New York: Simon and Schuster, 1961.

———. *The Story of Civilization, Part 8: The Age of Louis XIV*. New York: MJF Books, 1991.

———. *The Story of Civilization, Part 9: The Age of Voltaire*. New York: MJF Books, 1992.

———. *The Story of Civilization, Part 10: Rousseau and Revolution*. New York: MJF Books, 1967.

———. *The Story of Civilization, Part 11: The Age of Napoleon.* New York: MJF Books, 1975.

Embassy of the United States, Budapest, Hungary. Website: http://budapest.usembassy.gov/immigrant_application.html, 2007.

EUbusiness. Website: http://www.eubusiness.com/, 2007.

European Commission. Website: http://ec.europa.eu/, 2007.

European Union: Delegation of the European Commission to the United States. Website: http://www.eurunion.org/, 2007.

Frost, S. E., Jr. *Basic Teachings of the Great Philosophers.* New York: First Anchor Books, 1989.

Fukuyama, Francis. *America at the Crossroads: Democracy, Power, and the Neoconservative Legacy.* New Haven: Yale University Press, 2006.

———. *The End of History and the Last Man.* New York: The Free Press, 1992.

———. *The Great Disruption.* New York: The Free Press, 1999.

———. *Our Posthuman Future.* New York: Farrar, Straus, and Giroux, 2002.

———. *Trust: The Social Virtues and the Creation of Prosperity.* New York: The Free Press, 1995.

Gedmin, Jeffrey. "Europe and NATO: Saving the Alliance" in *Present Dangers.* San Francisco: Encounter Books, 2000.

German Embassy, Washington D.C. *The Euro.* Website: http://www.germany.info/relaunch/info/publications/infocus/euro/essentials.html.

Heisbourg, Francois. *La fin de l'Occident?* Paris: Odile Jacob, 2005.

Hüfner, Martin. *Europa: Die Macht von morgen.* München: Carl Hanser Verlag, 2006.

Huntington, Samuel P. *The Clash of Civilizations and the Remaking of World Order.* New York: Simon & Schuster, 1997.

——. *Who Are We?* New York: Simon & Schuster, 2004.

Immigration Service Center. "Immigrant Visas." Website: http://www.infodomain.com/immigran2.htm, 2007.

InfoPlease: All the Knowledge You Need. "Freedom in the World 2005." Website: http://www.infoplease.com/ipa/A0930918.html, 2007.

——. "The World's Most Repressive Societies." Website: http://www.infoplease.com/ipa/A0933891.html, 2007.

International Paneuropean Union. Website: http://www.paneuropa.org/, 2007.

Jacobs, Jane. *Dark Age Ahead.* New York: Random House, 2004.

Johnston, William M. *The Austrian Mind: An Intellectual and Social History 1848-1938.* Berkeley: University of California Press, 2000.

Kagan, Robert. *Dangerous Nation.* New York: Alfred A. Knopf, 2006.

——. *Of Paradise and Power: America and Europe in the New World Order.* New York: Alfred A. Knopf, 2003.

Kagan, Robert, and William Kristol, ed. *Present Dangers.* San Francisco: Encounter Books, 2000.

Kant, Immanuel. *Perpetual Peace: A Philosophical Sketch.* 1795. Website: http://www.mtholyoke.edu/acad/intrel/kant/kant1.htm, 2007.

Kennedy, Paul. *The Rise and Fall of the Great Powers.* New York: Vintage Books, 1989.

Kerr, Walter. *The Decline of Pleasure.* New York: Simon and Schuster, 1962.

Laphman, Lewis, and Peter T. Struck,eds. *The End of the World.* New York: St. Martin's Press, 1997.

Lloyd, Martin. *The Passport: The History of Man's Most Travelled Document.* Phoenix Mill Thrupp: Sutton Publishing Limited, 2003.

Marx, Karl, and Friedrich Engels, *The Communist Manifesto.* New York: Oxford University Press, 1998.

Markham, Felix. *Napoleon.* New York: New American Library, 1966.

Mazlish, Bruce. *Civilization and Its Contents.* Stanford: Stanford University Press, 2004.

Munro, Ross H. "China: The Challenge of a Rising Power" in *Present Dangers.* San Francisco: Encounter Books, 2000.

Nietzsche, Friedrich Wilhelm, ed. Walter Kaufmann. "Beyond Good and Evil: Prelude to a Philosophy of the Future" in *Basic Writings of Nietzsche.* New York: Modern Library Edition, 1992.

————. *The Portable Nietzsche.* New York: Penguin Books, 1982.

North Atlantic Treaty Organization (NATO). *The North Atlantic Treaty.* Washington D.C.: NATO, 1949. Website: http://www.nato.int/docu/basictxt/treaty. htm, 2007.

Organization of African Unity (OAU), Heads of State and Government of the Member States of the OAU. *Treaty Establishing the African Economic Community.* Abuja, Nigeria: 1991. Website: http://www.

nimdregionalforum.org/Portals/3/Treaty%20Establi
shing%20the%20African%20Economic%20Comm
unity.pdf, 2007.

Organization for Economic Co-operation and
Development (OECD). Website : http://www.oecd.
org/, 2007.

Ortega y Gasset, José. *The Dehumanization of Art and
other Writings on Art and Culture.* Garden City, N.Y.:
Doubleday Anchor Books, 1956

———. *An Interpretation of Universal History.* New York:
W.W. Norton & Company, 1973.

———. *The Revolt of the Masses.* New York: W.W. Norton
and Company, 1993.

———. *Toward a Philosophy of History.* New York: W. W.
Norton & Company, 1941.

Pinder, John. *The European Union: A Very Short
Introduction.* New York: Oxford University Press,
2001.

Reid, T.R. *The United States of Europe: The New
Superpower and the End of American Supremacy.* New
York: Penguin Books, 2004.

Rifkin, Jeremy. *The European Dream: How Europe's Vision
of the Future Is Quietly Eclipsing the American Dream.*
New York: Jeremy P. Tarcher/Penguin, 2004.

RTR, *Der Tagesspiegel.* Berlin/Brandenburg, Germany:
January 26, 2007.

Schiller, Johann Christoph Friedrich von. *Aesthetical and
Philosophical Essays.* New York: P. F. Collier & Son,
1902.

———. *Die Braut von Messina.* Salt Lake City: Project
Gutenberg Literary Archive Foundation, 2004.
Website: http://www.gutenberg.org/etext/6496,
2007.

————. "Letters upon the Aestetic Education on Man," *Literary Philosophical Essays*. New York: 1910.

Schiller, Friedrich, and Frederick Ungar, ed. and introduction. *An Anthology of Our Time*. New York: Frederick Ungar Publishing Co., 1960.

Schnabel, Rockwell A., and Francis X. Rocca. *The Next Superpower?: The Rise of Europe and its Challenge to the United States*. New York: Rowman & Littlefield Publisher, 2005.

Schuman, Robert. *Schuman Declaration*. Paris: 1950. Website: http://www.diplomatie.gouv.fr/archives.gb/dossiers/schuman/module03_4.html, 2007.

Spengler, Oswald. *The Decline of the West, Vol. 1*. New York: Alfred A. Knopf, 1926.

————. *The Decline of the West, Vol. 2*. New York: Alfred A. Knopf, 1928.

————. *The Decline of the West*. New York: Oxford University Press, 1991

Strayer, Joseph R., ed. *The Interpretation of History*. New York: Princeton University Press, 1950.

Toynbee, Arnold Joseph. "Art: Communicative or Esoteric?" *On the Future of Art*. New York: The Viking Press, 1970.

————. *Change and Habit: The Challenge of Our Time*. New York: Oxford University Press, 1966.

————. *Civilization on Trial & The World and the West*. New York: Meridian Books, 1958.

————. *Mankind and Mother Earth: A Narrative History of the World*. New York: Oxford University Press, 1976.

————. *A Study of History*. New York: Weathervane Books, 1972.

———. *War and Civilization.* Oxford: Oxford University Press, 1950.

The TransAtlantic Business Dialogue (TABD). Website: http://www.tabd.com/, 2007.

———. "Towards a Barrier-Free Transatlantic Market: Report and Recommendations to the 2006 EU-US Summit Leaders." Website: http://www.tabd.com/, 2007.

———. *U.S.–EU Economic Ministerial: TABD Submission to Governments, December 7, 2006*: "TABD November 2006, U.S.–EU Economic Ministerial Meeting." Website: http://www.tabd.com/, 2007.

Trans Atlantic Consumer Dialogue (TACD). Website: http://www.tacd.org, 2007.

U.S. Census 2000. Website: www.census.gov/prod/2004pubs/c2kbr-35.pdf, 2007.

Voltaire, Francois Marie Arouet de, and André Maurois, appreciation. *Candide,* Bantam Books, 1981.

Voltaire, Francois Marie Arouet de, and Ben Ray Redman, ed. *The Portable Voltaire,* New York: Viking Penguin, 1977.

Webster's New Universal Unabridged Dictionary. New York: Barnes & Noble Books, 1996.

The White House: Office of the Press Secretary, June 26, 2004. "Fact Sheet: U.S.-EU Summit: Strengthening the Transatlantic Economic Partnership." Website: http://www.whitehouse.gov/news/releases/2004/06/20040626-7.html, 2007.

Wikipedia: The Free Encyclopedia. Website: http://en.wikipedia.org/wiki/Main_Page, 2007.

The **AmEuropa**™ Series by

Kent M. Chater

Non-Fiction

AmEuropa: The Future of the West and The

Next Superpower

Fiction

AmEuropa: Love and Betrayal in the Greatest

Alliance of Nations